MISSISSIPPI

Real Estate License Law and Administrative Rules

Real Estate Training Institute

ISBN: 10:1519369514
ISBN-13: 978-1519369512

CONTENTS

TITLE 73. PROFESSIONS AND VOCATIONS CHAPTER 35. REAL ESTATE BROKERS IN GENERAL

§ 73-35-1. Citation of chapter; license requirement

This chapter shall be known, and may be cited, as "the Real Estate Brokers License Law of 1954"; and from and after May 6, 1954, it shall be unlawful for any person, partnership, association or corporation to engage in or carry on, directly or indirectly, or to advertise or to hold himself, itself or themselves out as engaging in or carrying on the business, or act in the capacity of, a real estate broker, or a real estate salesperson, within this state, without first obtaining a license as a real estate broker or real estate salesperson as provided for in this chapter.

§ 73-35-3. Definitions; applicability of chapter

(1) The term "real estate broker" within the meaning of this chapter shall include all persons, partnerships, associations and corporations, foreign and domestic, who for a fee, commission or other valuable consideration, or who with the intention or expectation of receiving or collecting the same, list, sell, purchase, exchange, rent, lease, manage or auction any real estate, or the improvements thereon, including options; or who negotiate or attempt to negotiate any such activity; or who advertise or hold themselves out as engaged in such activities; or who direct or assist in the procuring of a purchaser or prospect calculated or intended to result in a real estate transaction.

The term "real estate broker" shall also include any person, partnership, association or corporation employed by or on behalf of the owner or owners of lots or other parcels of real estate, at a stated salary or upon fee, commission or otherwise, to sell such real estate, or parts thereof, in lots or other parcels, including timesharing and condominiums, and who shall sell, exchange or lease, or offer or attempt or agree to negotiate the sale, exchange or lease of, any such lot or parcel of real estate.

(2) The term "real estate" as used in this chapter shall include leaseholds as well as any and every interest or estate in land, including timesharing and condominiums, whether corporeal or incorporeal, freehold or nonfreehold, and whether said property is situated in this state or elsewhere; provided, however, that the term "real estate" as used in this chapter shall not include oil, gas or mineral leases, nor shall it include any other mineral leasehold, mineral estate or mineral interest of any nature whatsoever.

(3) One (1) act in consideration of or with the expectation or intention of, or upon the promise of, receiving compensation, by fee, commission or otherwise, in the performance of any act or activity contained in subsection (1) of this section, shall constitute such person, partnership, association or corporation a real estate broker and make him, them or it subject to the provisions and requirements of this chapter.

(4) The term "real estate salesperson" shall mean and include any person employed or engaged by or on behalf of a licensed real estate broker to do or deal in any activity as included or comprehended by the definitions of a real estate broker in subsection (1) of this section, for compensation or otherwise.

(5) The term "automated valuation method" means any computerized model used by mortgage originators and secondary market issuers to determine the collateral worth of a mortgage secured by a consumer's principal dwelling.

(6) The term "broker price opinion" means an estimate prepared by a real estate broker, agent, or salesperson that details the probable selling price of a particular piece of real estate property and provides a varying level of detail about the property's condition, market, and neighborhood, and information on comparable sales, but does not include an automated valuation model.

(7) Exempt from the licensing requirements of this chapter shall be any person, partnership, association or corporation, who, as a bona fide owner, shall perform any aforesaid act with reference to property owned by them, or to the regular employees thereof who are on a stated salary, where such acts are performed in the regular course of business.

(8) The provisions of this chapter shall not apply to:

(a) Attorneys at law in the performance of primary or incidental duties as such attorneys at law.

(b) Any person holding in good faith a duly executed power of attorney from the owner, authorizing the final consummation and execution for the sale, purchase, leasing or exchange of real estate.

(c) The acts of any person while acting as a receiver, trustee, administrator, executor, guardian or under court order, or while acting under authority of a deed of trust or will.

(d) Public officers while performing their duties as such.

(e) Anyone dealing exclusively in oil and gas leases and mineral rights.

(9) Nothing in this chapter shall be construed to prohibit life insurance companies and their representatives from negotiating or attempting to negotiate loans secured by mortgages on real estate, nor shall these companies or their representatives be required to qualify as real estate brokers or agents under this chapter.

(10) The provisions of this chapter shall not apply to the activities of mortgagees approved by the Federal Housing Administration or the United States Department of Veterans Affairs, banks chartered under the laws of the State of Mississippi or the United States, savings and loan associations chartered under the laws of the State of Mississippi or the United States, licensees under the Small Loan Regulatory Law, being Sections 75-67-101 through 75-67-135, and under the Small Loan Privilege Tax Law, being Sections 75-67-

201 through 75-67-243, small business investment companies licensed by the Small Business Administration and chartered under the laws of the State of Mississippi, or any of their affiliates and subsidiaries, related to the making of a loan secured by a lien on real estate or to the disposing of real estate acquired by foreclosure or in lieu of foreclosure or otherwise held as security. No director, officer or employee of any such financial institution shall be required to qualify as a real estate broker or agent under this chapter when engaged in the aforesaid activities for and on behalf of such financial institution.

§ 73-35-4. Broker's price opinion; preparation, contents and use of opinion

(1) A person licensed under this chapter may prepare a broker's price opinion and charge and collect a fee for such opinion if:
(a) The license of that licensee is active and in good standing; and
(b) The broker's price opinion meets the requirements of subsections (3) and (4) of this section.

(2) Notwithstanding any provision to the contrary, a person licensed under this chapter may prepare a broker's price opinion for:

(a) An existing or potential seller for the purposes of listing and selling a parcel of real property;

(b) An existing or potential buyer of a parcel of real property;

(c) A third party making decisions or performing due diligence related to the potential listing, offering, sale, exchange, option, lease or acquisition price of a parcel of real property; or

(d) An existing or potential lienholder or other third party for any purpose other than as the basis to determine the value of a parcel of real property, for a mortgage loan origination, including first and second mortgages, refinances, or equity lines of credit.

(e) The provisions of this subsection do not preclude the preparation of a broker's price opinion to be used in conjunction with or in addition to an appraisal.

(3) A broker's price opinion prepared under the authority granted in this section shall be in writing and shall conform to the standards and guidelines published by a nationally recognized association of providers of broker price opinions. The Mississippi Real Estate Commission shall promulgate regulations that are consistent with, but not limited to, the standards and guidelines of a nationally recognized association of providers of broker price opinions.

(4) A broker's price opinion shall be in writing and contain the following:

(a) A statement of the intended purpose of the price opinion;

(b) A brief description of the subject property and property interest to be priced;

(c) The basis of reasoning used to reach the conclusion of the price, including the applicable market data and/or capitalization computation;

(d) Any assumptions or limiting conditions;

(e) A disclosure of any existing or contemplated interest of the broker or salesperson issuing the opinion;

(f) The effective date of the price opinion;

(g) The name and signature of the broker or salesperson issuing the price opinion;

(h) The name of the real estate brokerage firm for which the broker or salesperson is acting;

(i) The signature date;

(j) A disclaimer stating that, "This opinion is not an appraisal of the market value of the property, and may not be used in lieu of an appraisal. If an appraisal is desired, the services of a licensed or certified appraiser must be obtained. This opinion may not be used by any party as the primary basis to determine the value of a parcel of real property for a mortgage loan origination, including first and second mortgages, refinances or equity lines of credit.";

(k) A certification that the licensee is covered by errors and omissions insurance, to the extent required by state law, for all liability associated with the preparation of the broker's price opinion.

(5) If a broker's price opinion is submitted electronically or on a form supplied by the requesting party: (a) A signature required by paragraph (g) of subsection

(4) may be an electronic signature, as defined in Section 75-12-3. (b) A signature required by paragraph (g) of subsection (4) and the disclaimer required by paragraph (j) of subsection (4) may be transmitted in a separate attachment if the electronic format or form supplied by the requesting party does not allow additional comments to be written by the licensee. The electronic format or the form supplied by the requesting party must:

(i) Reference the existence of a separate attachment; and

(ii) Include a statement that the broker's price opinion is not complete without the attachment.

(6) Notwithstanding any provisions to the contrary, a person licensed pursuant to this chapter may not prepare a broker's price opinion for any purpose in lieu of an appraisal when an appraisal is required by federal or state statute. A broker's price opinion which estimates value or worth of a parcel of real estate rather than sales price shall be deemed to be an appraisal and may not be prepared by a licensed broker or sales agent under the authority of their

licensee but may only be prepared by a duly licensed appraiser and must meet the regulations promulgated by the Mississippi Real Estate Appraiser Licensing and Certification Board. A broker's price opinion may not under any circumstances be referred to as a valuation or appraisal.

§ 73-35-4.1. Disclosure of information concerning size or area of property involved in real estate transaction; liability; remedy for violation of section

(1) (a) In connection with any real estate transaction, the size or area, in square footage or otherwise, of the subject property, if provided by any real estate licensee in accordance with paragraph

(b)(i) and (ii), shall not be considered any warranty or guarantee of the size or area information, in square footage or otherwise, of the subject property.

(b) (i) If a real estate licensee provides any party to a real estate transaction with third-party information concerning the size or area, in square footage or otherwise, of the subject property involved in the transaction, the licensee shall identify the source of the information.

(ii) For the purposes of this section, "third-party information" means: 1. An appraisal or any measurement information prepared by a licensed appraiser;

2. A surveyor developer's plan prepared by a licensed surveyor;

3. A tax assessor's public record; or

4. A builder's plan used to construct or market the property.

(c) A real estate licensee has no duty to the seller or purchaser of real property to conduct an independent investigation of the size or area, in square footage or otherwise, of a subject property, or to independently verify the accuracy of any third-party information.

(d) A real estate licensee who has complied with the requirements of this section, as applicable, shall have no further duties to the seller or purchaser of real property regarding disclosed or undisclosed property size or area information, and shall not be subject to liability to any party for any damages sustained with regard to any conflicting measurements or opinions of size or area, including exemplary or punitive damages.

(2) (a) If a real estate licensee has provided third-party information to any party to a real estate transaction concerning size or area of the subject real property, a party to the real estate transaction may recover damages from the licensee in a civil action only when a licensee knowingly violates the duty to disclose the source of the information as required in this section. However, nothing in this section shall provide immunity from civil liability to any licensee who knowingly misrepresents the size or area of the subject real property.

(b) The sole and exclusive civil remedy at common law or otherwise for a violation of this section by a real estate licensee shall be an action for actual damages suffered by the party as a result of such violation and shall not include exemplary or punitive damages.

(c) For any real estate transaction commenced after July 1, 2013, any civil action brought pursuant to this section shall be commenced within two (2) years after the date of transfer of the subject real property.

(d) In any civil action brought pursuant to this section, the prevailing party shall be allowed court costs and reasonable attorney fees to be set by the court and collected as costs of the action.

(e) A transfer of a possessory interest in real property subject to the provisions of this section may not be invalidated solely because of the failure of any person to comply with the provisions of this section.

(f) The provisions of this section shall apply to, regulate and determine the rights, duties, obligations and remedies, at common law or otherwise, of the seller marketing the seller's real property for sale through a real estate licensee, and of the purchaser of real property offered for sale through a real estate licensee, with respect to disclosure of third-party information concerning the subject real property's size or area, in square footage or otherwise, and this section hereby supplants and abrogates all common-law liability, rights, duties, obligations and remedies of all parties therefor.

§ 73-35-5. Real estate commission created; organization; seal; records

(1) There is hereby created the Mississippi Real Estate Commission.

The commission shall consist of five (5) persons, to be appointed by the Governor with the advice and consent of the Senate. Each appointee shall have been a resident and citizen of this state for at least six (6) years prior to his appointment, and his vocation for at least five (5) years shall have been that of a real estate broker. One (1) member shall be appointed for the term of one (1) year; two (2) members for terms of two (2) years; two (2) members for terms of four (4) years; thereafter, the term of the members of said commission shall be for four (4) years and until their successors are appointed and qualify.

There shall be at least one (1) commissioner from each congressional district, as such districts are constituted as of July 1, 2002. The commissioners appointed from each of the congressional districts shall be bona fide residents of the district from which each is appointed. One (1) additional commissioner shall be appointed without regard to residence in any particular congressional district.

Members to fill vacancies shall be appointed by the Governor for the unexpired term. The Governor may remove any commissioner for cause. The State of Mississippi shall not be required to furnish office space for such commissioners. The provisions of this section shall not affect persons who are members of the Real Estate Commission as of January 1, 2002. Such members shall serve out their respective terms, upon the expiration of which the provisions of this section shall take effect.

Nothing provided herein shall be construed as prohibiting the reappointment of any member of the said commission.

(2) The commission shall organize by selecting from its members a chairman, and may do all things necessary and convenient for carrying into effect the provisions of this chapter, and may from time to time promulgate rules and regulations. Each member of the commission shall receive per diem as authorized in Section 25-3-69, Mississippi Code of 1972, and his actual and necessary expenses incurred in the performance of duties pertaining to his office as authorized in Section 25-3-41, Mississippi Code of 1972. (3) The commission shall adopt a seal by which it shall authenticate its proceedings. Copies of all records and papers in the office of the commission, duly certified and authenticated by the seal of said commission, shall be received in evidence in all courts equally and with like effect as the original. All records kept in the office of the commission under authority of this chapter shall be open to public inspection except pending investigative files.

§ 73-35-6. Licenses for business entities

A corporation, partnership, company or association shall be granted a license when individual broker's licenses have been issued to every member, owner, partner or officer of such partnership, company, association or corporation who actively participates in its brokerage business and when any required fee is paid.

§ 73-35-7. Qualifications for license

Licenses shall be granted only to persons who present, and to corporations, partnerships, companies or associations whose officers, associates or partners present satisfactory proof to the commission that they are trustworthy and competent to transact the business of a real estate broker or real estate salesperson in such manner as to safeguard the interests of the public. Every person who applies for a resident license as a real estate broker:

(a) shall be age twenty-one (21) years or over, and have his legal domicile in the State of Mississippi at the time he applies;

(b) shall be subject to the jurisdiction of this state, subject to the income tax laws and other excise laws thereof, subject to the road and bridge privilege tax laws thereof;

(c) shall not be an elector in any other state;

(d) shall have held a license as an active real estate salesperson for twelve (12) months immediately prior to making application for the broker's examination hereafter specified;

(e) shall have successfully completed a minimum of one hundred twenty (120) hours of courses in real estate as hereafter specified; and

(f) shall have successfully completed the real estate broker's examination as hereafter specified; and

(g) shall have successfully been cleared for licensure by the commission's background investigation as provided in Section 73-35-10.

An applicant who has not held an active real estate salesperson's license for a period of at least twelve (12) months immediately prior to submitting an application shall have successfully completed a minimum of one hundred fifty (150) classroom hours in real estate courses, which courses are acceptable for credit toward a degree at a college or university as approved by the Southern Association of Colleges and Schools.

Every applicant for a resident license as a real estate salesperson shall be age eighteen (18) years or over, shall be a bona fide resident of the State of Mississippi prior to filing his application, and shall have successfully completed a minimum of sixty (60) hours in courses in real estate as hereafter specified; and shall have successfully completed the real estate salesperson's examination as hereafter specified.

The residency requirements set forth in this section shall not apply to those licensees of other states who qualify and obtain nonresident licenses in this state.

The commission is authorized to exempt from such prelicensing educational requirements, in whole or in part, a real estate licensee of another state who desires to obtain a license under this Rev. 10/2016

chapter; provided, however, that the prelicensing educational requirements in the other state are determined by the commission to be equivalent to prelicensing educational requirements in this state and provided that such state extends this same privilege or exemption to Mississippi real estate licensees. The issuance of a license by reciprocity to a military-trained applicant or military spouse shall be subject to the provisions of Section 73-50-1.

§ 73-35-8. Nonresident's license; application

(1) A nonresident may apply for a nonresident's license in Mississippi provided the individual is

(i) a licensed broker in another state or

(ii) is a broker/salesperson or salesperson affiliated with a resident or nonresident Mississippi broker or

(iii) is a nonresident who applies for a broker's license and who will maintain an office in Mississippi. The nonresident broker need not maintain a place of business within Mississippi provided he is regularly actively engaged in the real estate business and maintains a place of business in the other state. The nonresident licensee or applicant shall be subject to all the provisions of this chapter except for the residency requirement and approved equivalent pre-licensing education.

(2) Every nonresident applicant shall file a statement of irrevocable consent with the Real Estate Commission that legal actions may be commenced against him in the proper court of any county of this state in which a cause of action may arise or in which the plaintiff may reside by service of process or pleading authorized by the laws of this state, by the Secretary of State of Mississippi, or by any member of the commission or chief executive officer thereof, the consent stipulating that the service of process or pleading shall be taken in all courts to be valid and binding as if personal service had been made upon the nonresident licensee in this state. The consent shall be duly acknowledged. Every nonresident licensee shall consent to have any hearings conducted by the commission pursuant to Section 73-35-23, Mississippi Code of 1972, at a place designated by the commission.

(3) Any service of process or pleading shall be served on the executive officer of the commission by filing duplicate copies, one (1) of which shall be filed in the office of the commission and the other forwarded by certified mail to the last known principal address of the nonresident licensee against whom such process or pleading is directed. No default in any such action shall be taken except upon an affidavit of certification of the commission or the executive officer thereof that a copy of the process or pleading was mailed to the defendant as herein provided, and no default judgment shall be taken in any such action or proceeding until thirty (30) days after the mailing of process or pleading to the defendant.

(4) An applicant shall sign an agreement to cooperate with any investigation of the applicant's real estate brokerage activities which the commission may undertake.

(5) Each applicant for a nonresident license must qualify in all respects, including education, examination and fees, as an applicant who is a resident of Mississippi with the exception of the residency requirement and approved equivalent prelicensing education.

(6) A certification from the Executive Officer of the Real Estate Commission in the state in which the nonresident maintains his principal place of business shall be required.

An applicant
shall disclose all states in which he has held a real estate license and furnish a certification of licensure from that state or states.

(7) The applicant/broker shall obtain an appropriate Mississippi license for the firm through which he intends to operate as a broker.

(8) Any nonresident broker, broker-salesperson and salesperson shall meet Mississippi continuing education requirements after becoming licensed just as any resident licensee.

(9) A broker or salesperson licensed in this state, on inactive status in good standing and no longer a resident of this state, may, after meeting other requirements for nonresident licensees, make application for a nonresident license without being required to meet current prelicensing educational requirements at the time of application or having to sit for the examination in order to obtain the equivalent nonresident license.

(10) A nonresident licensee in good standing who changes his legal domicile to the State of Mississippi may obtain a resident license equivalent to his nonresident license without meeting the current educational requirements or sitting for the examination, provided other requirements set forth for residents of the state are met.

(11) A nonresident licensee may utilize the inactive status for his license under the same requirements as a resident licensee,

including but not limited to, continuing education requirements and ceasing active status under a licensed nonresident broker.

§ 73-35-9. Application for license

(1) Every applicant for a real estate broker's license shall apply therefor in writing upon blanks prepared by the commission and shall provide such data and information as the commission may require.

(2) Such application shall be accompanied by the recommendation of at least three

(3) citizens who have been property owners for at least three (3) years, who have known the applicant for three (3) years, and who are not related to the applicant, certifying that the applicant bears a good reputation for honesty and trustworthiness and recommending that a license be granted to the applicant. (3) Every applicant for a salesperson's license shall apply therefor in writing upon blanks prepared by the commission and shall provide such data and information as the commission may require.

(4) Each application for license shall also be accompanied by two (2) photographs of the applicant in such form as the commission may prescribe. (5) Each application or filing made under this section shall include the social security number(s) of the applicant in accordance with Section 93-11-64, Mississippi Code of 1972.

§ 73-35-10. Background investigation required of applicants for real estate broker's, real estate salesperson's, or nonresident's license Rev. 10/2016

§ 73-35-10. Background investigation required of applicants for real estate broker's, real estate salesperson's, or nonresident's license

(1) (a) To qualify for a Mississippi real estate broker's license or a Mississippi resident license as a real estate salesperson, or a

nonresident's license in Mississippi, an applicant must have successfully been cleared for licensure through an investigation that shall consist of a determination that the applicant does not possess a background which calls into question public trust, as set forth below in subsection (2), and verification that the prospective licensee is not guilty of or in violation of any statutory ground for denial of licensure as set forth in Section 73-35-21.

(b) To assist the commission in conducting its licensure investigation, from and after July 1, 2016, all applicants for a Mississippi real estate broker's license, or a Mississippi resident license as a real estate salesperson, or a nonresident's license in Mississippi, and all applicants for renewal of any real estate license shall undergo a fingerprint-based criminal history records check of the Mississippi central criminal database and the Federal Bureau of Investigation criminal history database. Each applicant shall submit a full set of the applicant's fingerprints in a form and manner prescribed by the commission, which shall be forwarded to the Mississippi Department of Public Safety (department) and the Federal Bureau of Investigation Identification Division for this purpose.

(c) Any and all state or national criminal history records information obtained by the commission that is not already a matter of public record shall be deemed nonpublic and confidential information restricted to the exclusive use of the commission, its members, officers, investigators, agents and attorneys in evaluating the applicant's eligibility or disqualification for licensure, and shall be exempt from the Mississippi Public Records Act of 1983. Except when introduced into evidence in a hearing before the commission to determine licensure, no such information or records related thereto shall, except with the written consent of the applicant or by order of a court of competent jurisdiction, be released or otherwise disclosed by the commission to any other person or agency.

(d) The commission shall provide to the department the fingerprints of the applicant, any additional information that may be required by the department, and a form signed by the applicant consenting to the check of the criminal records and to the use of the fingerprints and other identifying information required by the state or national repositories.

(e) The commission shall charge and collect from the applicant, in addition to all other applicable fees and costs, such amount as may be incurred by the commission in requesting and obtaining state and national criminal history records information on the applicant. (2) (a) The commission must ensure that applicants for real estate licenses do not possess a background that could call into question public trust. An applicant found by the commission to possess a background which calls into question the applicant's ability to maintain public trust shall not be issued a real estate license. (b) The commission shall not issue a real estate license if:

(i) The applicant has had a real estate license revoked in any governmental jurisdiction within the five-year period immediately preceding the date of the application;

(ii) The applicant has been convicted of, or pled guilty or nolo contendere to, a felony in a domestic or foreign court:

1. During the five-year period immediately preceding the date of the application for licensing; or

2. At any time preceding the date of the application, if such felony involved an act of fraud, dishonesty or a breach of trust, or money laundering.

(c) The commission shall adopt rules and regulations necessary to implement, administer and enforce the provisions of this section.

(d) The requirement of a criminal background check provided in this section shall not apply to persons who have held a broker's or salesperson's license in this state for at least twenty-five (25) years and who are older than seventy (70) years of age.

§ 73-35-11. Nonresident may not act except in cooperation with licensed broker of state

It shall be unlawful for any licensed broker, salesperson or other person who is not licensed as a Mississippi resident or nonresident broker or salesperson and a licensed broker or licensed salesperson in this state to perform any of the acts regulated by this chapter, except that a licensed broker of another state who does not hold a Mississippi real estate license may cooperate with a licensed broker of this state provided that any commission or fee resulting from such cooperative negotiation shall be stated on a form filed with the commission reflecting the compensation to be paid to the Mississippi broker.

Whenever a Mississippi broker enters into a cooperative agreement under this section, the Mississippi broker shall file within ten (10) days with the commission a copy of each such written agreement. By signing the agreement, the nonresident broker who is not licensed in this state agrees to abide by Mississippi law, and the rules and regulations of the commission; and further agrees that civil actions may be commenced against him in any court of competent jurisdiction in any county of this state in which a claim may arise.

The Mississippi broker shall require a listing or joint listing of the property involved. The written cooperative agreements shall specify all material terms of each agreement, including but not limited to its financial terms. The showing of property located in Mississippi and negotiations pertaining thereto shall be supervised by the Mississippi broker. In all advertising of real estate located in Mississippi, the name and telephone number of the Mississippi broker shall appear and shall be given equal prominence with the name of the nonresident broker who is not licensed in this state.

The Mississippi broker shall be liable for all acts of the above cooperating broker, as well as for his own acts, arising from the execution of any cooperative agreement. The Mississippi broker shall determine that the cooperating broker is licensed as a broker in another state. All earnest money pertaining to a cooperative agreement must be held in escrow by the Mississippi broker unless both the buyer and seller agree in writing to relieve the Mississippi broker of this responsibility.

§ 73-35-13. Written examination requirement; exemption for licensee of another state; reciprocity

(1) In addition to proof of his honesty, trustworthiness and good reputation, the applicant shall take a written examination which shall be held at least four (4) times each year at regular intervals and on stated times by the commission and shall test reading, writing, spelling, elementary arithmetic and his general knowledge of the statutes of this state relating to real property, deeds, mortgages, agreements of sale, agency, contract, leases, ethics, appraisals, the provisions of this chapter and such other matters the commission certifies as necessary to the practice of real estate brokerage in the State of Mississippi. The examination for a broker's license shall differ from the examination for a salesperson's license, in that it shall be of a more exacting nature and require higher standards of knowledge of real estate. The commission shall cause examinations to be conducted at such times and places as it shall determine.

(2) In event the license of any real estate broker or salesperson is revoked by the commission subsequent to the enactment of this chapter, no new license shall be issued to such person unless he complies with the provisions of this chapter.

(3) No person shall be permitted or authorized to act as a real estate broker or salesperson until he has qualified by examination, except as hereinbefore provided. Any individual who fails to pass the examination for salesperson upon two (2) occasions, shall be ineligible for a similar examination, until after the expiration of three (3) months from the time such individual last took the examination. Any individual who fails to pass the broker's examination upon two (2) occasions, shall be ineligible for a similar examination until after the expiration of six (6) months

from the time such individual last took the examination, and then only upon making application as in the first instance.

(4) If the applicant is a partnership, association or corporation, said examination shall be taken on behalf of said partnership, association or corporation by the member or officer thereof who is designated in the application as the person to receive a license by virtue of the issuing of a license to such partnership, association or corporation.

(5) Upon satisfactorily passing such examination and upon complying with all other provisions of law and conditions of this chapter, a license shall thereupon be issued to the successful applicant who, upon receiving such license, is authorized to conduct the business of a real estate broker or real estate salesperson in this state.

(6) The commission is authorized to exempt from such examination, in whole or in part, a real estate licensee of another state who desires to obtain a license under this chapter; provided, however, that the examination administered in the other state is determined by the commission to be equivalent to such examination given in this state and provided that such other state extends this same privilege or exemption to Mississippi real estate licensees. The issuance of a license by reciprocity to a military-trained applicant or military spouse shall be subject to the provisions of Section 73-50-1.

§ 73-35-14. Real estate schools; regulation by commission

(1) An institution or organization desiring to conduct a school or offer a course of instruction to prepare persons to be licensed under this chapter, or to offer post-licensure courses, shall apply to the commission for accreditation, and shall submit evidence that it is prepared to carry out a prescribed minimum curriculum in real estate principles and practices as set forth in this chapter and can meet other standards established by the commission. An investigation of the school and of the institution or organization

with which such school is affiliated shall be made by the commission. If, in the opinion of the commission, the requirements for an accredited school for instruction in real estate principles and practices are met, the commission shall approve the school as an accredited real estate school upon payment of the fees set forth in this chapter and such other fees as established by the commission. All schools so accredited shall register at required intervals on a form provided and pay the required registration fees specified in this chapter and such other fees as established by the commission.

(2) The commission shall have the authority to revoke, suspend or otherwise discipline the accreditation of any real estate school, prelicense education provider or post-license education provider if the commission determines that the school or education provider is not meeting or has not met the standards required for such accreditation. If the commission determines that any accredited real estate school or education provider is not maintaining the standards required by the commission, notices thereof in writing specifying the defect or defects shall be given promptly to the school or provider. If such defect or defects are not remedied in the time specified by the commission, the commission shall hold a hearing to determine the disciplinary action, if any, to be taken. Such hearing will be noticed to the school or provider, who will be allowed to attend the hearing and present to the commission its reasons why it should not be disciplined.

(3) A college or university in the State of Mississippi accredited by the Southern Association of Colleges and Schools or the comparable regional accrediting authority shall be an approved education provider for prelicense courses for both the broker's and salesperson's license by virtue of such accreditation. Such colleges and universities are not required to meet any other standards provided herein.

§ 73-35-14.1. Standards for real estate schools

(1) Minimum standards for initial and continuing accreditation as a real estate school or prelicense education provider shall include:

(a) Payment of any fees established by the commission. If the school or provider is accredited as a prelicense school or prelicense education provider, fees shall include a biennial fee of Two Thousand Five Hundred Dollars ($2,500.00).

(b) The school or prelicense education provider must maintain an annual average pass rate of at least sixty-five percent (65%) on each of the real estate broker's license examination and the real estate salesperson's license examination. The term annual average pass rate shall be as defined by the commission. If a school or prelicense education provider does not meet the minimum annual average pass rate, the commission shall allow the school or prelicense education provider a minimum of a three-month time period in which to attain the minimum annual average pass rate.

(c) Schools and prelicense education providers must use a method for instructor evaluation by students attending prelicense education classes. The commission may establish minimum standards for instructor evaluation. In the event the provider does not meet those minimum standards, the commission may revoke a provider's authority to offer prelicense education courses. Schools and prelicense education providers must provide the results of such instructor evaluations to the commission in the manner the commission directs.

(2) The commission may establish by rule such other standards for schools, prelicense education providers and post-license education providers as the commission may deem necessary.

§ 73-35-14.2. Standards for instructors

(1) Minimum standards for instructors for prelicense and post-license education courses required for licensure as a real estate broker or a real estate salesperson shall include:

(a) Licensure as a Mississippi real estate broker or real estate salesperson for the immediate past five (5) years prior to application; or

(b) Current certification as a Certified Public Accountant; or

(c) Attainment of a Juris Doctor (J.D.) or Bachelor of Laws (L.L.B.) degree from a law school whose accreditation is recognized by the Mississippi Supreme Court; or

(d) Demonstration of significant expertise in a particular real estate related subject area, as determined and approved by the Commission.

(2) The commission may establish by rule such other standards for instructors of prelicense education and post-license education as the commission may deem necessary.

§ 73-35-14.3. Course content

(1) Minimum standards for the content for education courses required for licensure as a real estate broker or a real estate salesperson shall include content on: Rev. 10/2016

(a) The provisions of this chapter and any rules and regulations promulgated hereunder;

(b) Listing property;

(c) Property valuation/appraisal;

(d) Real estate arithmetic;

(e) Characteristics of real property;

(f) Agency and nonagency relationships;

(g) Real estate sale contracts/agreements of sale;

(h) Leasing and property management;

(i) Transfer of title/ownership/deeds;

(j) Settlement procedures;

(k) Financing;

(*l*) Professional responsibilities and ethics;

(m) Fair housing; (n) Federal laws affecting real estate.

(2) A prelicense course must meet any standards that the Association of Real Estate Licensing Law Officials (ARELLO), or its successor(s), may have for prelicense courses, including, without limitation, standards for content, form, examination, facilities and instructors. If ARELLO or its successor(s) operate a certification program for prelicense courses, a prelicense course must be certified by ARELLO or its successor(s) before the commission may approve the course.

(3) The commission may establish by rule such other standards for prelicense education course content as the commission may deem necessary.

(4) No more than eight (8) prelicense hours may be earned in a single day.

(5) Courses covering the general content of subsection (1) of this section that are acceptable for credit toward a degree at a college or university as approved by the Southern Association of Colleges and Schools or the comparable regional accrediting authority shall qualify for the minimum standards for prelicense education by virtue of said accreditation. A semester-hour credit shall be equal to fifteen (15) classroom hours and a quarter-hour credit shall be equal to ten (10) classroom hours. Courses given under this section by such accredited institutions are not

required to meet ARELLO standards or certifications.

The commission may establish by rule that specific areas of the general content areas listed in subsection (1) of this section are not required to be met by courses offered by the accredited institutions under this subsection.

§ 73-35-14.4. Distance learning courses

(1) The term "distance learning course(s)" shall mean any course approved by the commission in which the student is not physically present in a classroom with the instructor, including, without limitation, correspondence courses, video/DVD based courses and online electronic courses.

(2) The commission may approve distance learning courses for prelicense education, post-license education and continuing education courses. Any distance learning course must meet any standards that the Association of Real Estate Licensing Law Officials (ARELLO), or its successor(s), may have for such courses, including, without limitation, standards for content, form, examination, facilities and instructors.

If no ARELLO standards exist for a distance learning course, the commission shall establish by rule such minimum standards. If ARELLO or its successor(s) operate a certification program for distance learning courses, a distance learning course must be certified by ARELLO or its successor(s) before the commission may approve the course.

§ 73-35-14.5. Temporary licenses; post-license education

(1) Upon passing the Mississippi broker's or salesperson's examination and complying with all other conditions for licensure, a temporary license shall be issued to the applicant. The fee for the temporary license shall also be the same for the permanent license as provided in Section 73-35-17.

A temporary license shall be valid for a period of one (1) year following the first day of the month after its issuance.

(2) All Mississippi residents who apply for and receive a nonresident Mississippi broker's or salesperson's license shall be subject to the requirements under this section, including temporary licensure and completion of a thirty-hour post-license course.

(3) The holder of a temporary license shall not be issued a permanent license until he has satisfactorily completed a thirty-hour post-license course prescribed by the commission and offered by providers specifically certified by the commission to offer this mandated post-license education. The holder of a temporary license shall complete the entire thirty-hour course within twelve (12) months of issuance of his temporary license; otherwise this temporary license shall automatically be placed on inactive status by the Mississippi Real Estate Commission. If the holder of the temporary license does not complete the course and have his permanent license issued within one (1) year following the first day of the month after its issuance, the temporary license shall automatically expire and lapse. A temporary license is not subject to renewal procedures in this chapter and may not be renewed.

(4) The thirty-hour post-license course shall be offered by providers certified and approved by the commission, and an annual certification fee of One Thousand Dollars ($1,000.00) shall be charged to providers. The thirty-hour post-license coursework shall be offered in no less than fifteen-hour increments of classroom instruction. No more than eight (8) hours may be earned in a single day. The commission shall determine standards for approval of post-license courses and course providers, and shall require certification of such coursework of the applicant. There shall be different content criteria for post-license education for salesperson licensees and for broker licensees. In the post-license course for salesperson licensees, a minimum of twenty-four (24) hours of the thirty-hour coursework shall be in the following subjects: agency relationships, contracts, earnest money, antitrust, fair housing, ethics and property condition disclosure. The remaining six (6)

hours shall be in subjects intended to enhance the competency of salesperson licensees in representing consumers, and may include the following subjects: pricing property, environmental issues, home inspections, leases and property management, and mortgage processes. In the post-license course for broker licensees, a minimum of twenty-four (24) hours of the thirty-hour coursework shall be in the following subjects: managing escrow accounts, intraoffice confidentiality, broker responsibilities to licensees, office policies and procedures (including agency office policies), broker agreements with licensees and assistants and Mississippi Real Estate Commission required forms and any other subject as the commission may, by rule, require to be included in such course. The remaining six (6) hours shall be in subjects intended to enhance the competency of brokers, including, without limitation, managing agents, recruiting, retention, budgeting and financial planning.

(5) The holder of an active license who has satisfactorily completed the post-license course and whose permanent license has been issued shall not be subject to the sixteen-hour continuing education requirement in this chapter for the first renewal of his permanent license.

§ 73-35-15. Location of business and responsible broker to be designated

(1) Every person, partnership, association or corporation licensed as a real estate broker shall be required to have and maintain a definite place of business, which shall be a room either in his home or an office elsewhere, to be used for the transaction of real estate business, or such business and any allied business. The certificate of registration as broker and the certificate of each real estate salesperson employed by such broker shall be prominently displayed in said office. The said place of business shall be designated in the license. In case of removal from the designated address, the licensee shall make application to the commission before removal, or within ten (10) days after removal, designating the new location of such office, whereupon the commission shall

forthwith issue a new license for the new location for the unexpired period.

(2) All licenses issued to a real estate salesperson or broker-salesperson shall designate the responsible broker of such salesperson or broker-salesperson. Prompt notice in writing, within three (3) days, shall be given to the commission by any real estate salesperson of a change of responsible broker, and of the name of the principal broker into whose agency the salesperson is about to enter; and a new license shall thereupon be issued by the commission to such salesperson for the unexpired term of the original license upon the return to the commission of the license previously issued. The change of responsible broker or employment by any licensed real estate salesperson without notice to the commission as required shall automatically cancel his license. Upon termination of a salesperson's agency, the responsible broker shall within three (3) days return the salesperson's license to the commission for cancellation. It shall be unlawful for any real estate salesperson to perform any of the acts contemplated by this chapter either directly or indirectly after his agency has been terminated and his license has been returned for cancellation until his license has been reissued by the commission.

§ 73-35-16. Real estate licensees required to obtain errors and omissions insurance coverage; persons required to submit proof of errors and omissions insurance; minimum requirements of group policy issued to commission; public bid for group insurance contract; requirements for independent coverage; rules and regulations

(1) The following words and phrases shall have the meanings ascribed herein unless the context clearly indicates otherwise:

(a) "Aggregate limit" means a provision in an insurance contract limiting the maximum liability of an insurer for a series of losses in a given time period such as the policy term.

(b) "Claims-made" means policies written under a claims-made basis which shall cover claims made (reported or filed) during the year the policy is in force for incidents which occur that year or during any previous period the policyholder was insured under the claims-made contract. This form of coverage is in contrast to the occurrence policy which covers today's incident regardless of when a claim is filed even if it is one or more years later. (c) "Extended reporting period" means a designated period of time after a claims-made policy has expired during which a claim may be made and coverage triggered as if the claim had been made during the policy period. (d) "Licensee" means any active individual broker, broker-salesperson or salesperson, any partnership or any corporation. (e) "Per-claim limit" means the maximum limit payable, per licensee, for damages arising out of the same error, omission or wrongful act. (f) "Prior acts coverage" applies to policies on a claims-made versus occurrence basis. Prior acts coverage responds to claims that are made during a current policy period, but the act or acts causing the claim or injuries for which the claim is made occurred prior to the inception of the current policy period. (g) "Proof of coverage" means a copy of the actual policy of insurance, a certificate of insurance or a binder of insurance. (h) "Retroactive date" means a provision, found in many claims-made policies, that the policy shall not cover claims for injuries or damages that occurred before the retroactive date even if the claim is first made during the policy period. (2) The following persons shall submit proof of insurance: (a) Any active individual broker, active broker-salesperson or active salesperson; Rev. 10/2016

(b) Any partnership (optional); or (c) Any corporation (optional). (3) Individuals whose licenses are on inactive status are not required to carry errors and omissions insurance. (4) All Mississippi licensees shall be covered for activities contemplated under this chapter. (5) Licensees may obtain errors and omissions coverage through the insurance carrier approved by the Mississippi Real Estate Commission and provided on a group policy basis. The following are minimum requirements of the group policy to be issued to the commission, including, as named insureds, all licensees who have paid their required premium: (a) All activities contemplated under this chapter are included as covered activities;

(b) A per-claim limit is not less than One Hundred Thousand Dollars ($100,000.00);

(c) An annual aggregate limit is not less than One Hundred Thousand Dollars ($100,000.00);

(d) Limits apply per licensee per claim;

(e) Maximum deductible is Two Thousand Five Hundred Dollars ($2,500.00) per licensee per claim for damages;

(f) Maximum deductible is One Thousand Dollars ($1,000.00) per licensee per claim for defense costs; and

(g) The contract of insurance pays, on behalf of the injured person(s), liabilities owed.

(6) (a) The maximum contract period between the insurance carrier and the commission is to be five (5) consecutive policy terms, after which time period the commission shall place the insurance out for competitive bid. The commission shall reserve the right to place the contract out for bid at the end of any policy period.

(b) The policy period shall be a twelve-month policy term. (c) The retroactive date for the master policy shall not be before July 1, 1994.

(i) The licensee may purchase full prior acts coverage on July 1, 1994, if the licensee can show proof of errors and omissions coverage that has been in effect since at least March 15, 1994.

(ii) If the licensee purchases full prior acts coverage on July 1, 1994, that licensee shall continue to be guaranteed full prior acts coverage if the insurance carriers are changed in the future.

(iii) If the licensee was not carrying errors and omissions insurance on July 1, 1994, the individual certificate shall be issued with a retroactive date of July 1, 1994. This date shall not be advanced if the insurance carriers are changed in the future.

(iv) For any new licensee who first obtains a license after July 1, 1994, the retroactive date shall be the effective date of licensure.

(v) For any licensee who changes status of license from inactive to active, the retroactive date shall be the effective date of change to "active" licensure.

(d) Each licensee shall be notified of the required terms and conditions of coverage for the policy at least thirty (30) days before the renewal date of the policy.

A certificate of coverage, showing compliance with the required terms and conditions of coverage, shall be filed with the commission by the renewal date of the policy by each licensee who elects not to participate in the insurance program administered by the commission.

(e) If the commission is unable to obtain errors and omissions insurance coverage to insure all licensees who choose to participate in the insurance program at a premium of no more than Two Hundred Fifty Dollars ($250.00) per twelve (12) months' policy period, the requirement of insurance coverage under this section shall be void during the applicable contract period.

(7) Licensees may obtain errors and omissions coverage independently if the coverage contained in the policy complies with the following minimum requirements:

(a) All activities contemplated under this chapter are included as covered activities;

(b) A per-claim limit is not less than One Hundred Thousand Dollars ($100,000.00);

(c) The deductible is not more than Two Thousand Five Hundred Dollars ($2,500.00) per licensee per claim for damages and the deductible is not more than One Thousand Dollars ($1,000.00) per licensee per claim for defense costs; and

(d) If other insurance is provided as proof of errors and omissions coverage, the other insurance carrier shall agree to a non-cancelable policy or to provide a letter of commitment to notify the commission thirty (30) days before the intention to cancel.

(8) The following provisions apply to individual licensees:

(a) The commission shall require receipt of proof of errors and omissions insurance from new licensees within thirty (30) days of licensure. Any licenses issued at any time other than policy renewal time shall be subject to a pro rata premium.

(b) For licensees not submitting proof of insurance necessary to continue active licensure, the commission shall be responsible for sending notice of deficiency to those licensees. Licensees who do not correct the deficiency within thirty (30) days shall have their licenses placed on inactive status. The commission shall assess fees for inactive status and for return to active status when errors and omissions insurance has been obtained.

(c) Any licensee insured in the state program whose license becomes inactive shall not be charged an additional premium if the license is reactivated during the policy period.

(9) The commission is authorized to adopt such rules and regulations as it deems appropriate to handle administrative duties relating to operation of the program, including billing and premium collection.

§ 73-35-17. Fees

(1) A fee not to exceed One Hundred Fifty Dollars ($150.00) shall accompany an application for a real estate broker's license, and in the event that the applicant successfully passes the examination, no

additional fee shall be required for the issuance of a license for a one-year period; provided, that if an applicant fails to pass the examination, he may be eligible to take the next or succeeding examination without the payment of an additional fee. In the event a contract testing service is utilized, the fee associated with administering the test shall be collected by the testing provider and the application fee for any real estate license shall be collected by the commission.

(2) For each license as a real estate broker issued to a member of a partnership, association or officer of a corporation other than the member or officer named in the license issued to such partnership, association or corporation, a fee not to exceed Seventy-five Dollars ($75.00) shall be charged.

(3) A fee not to exceed One Hundred Twenty Dollars ($120.00) shall accompany an application for a real estate salesperson's license, and in the event that the applicant successfully passes the examination, no additional fee shall be required for the issuance of a license for a one-year period; provided, that if an applicant fails to pass the examination, he may be eligible to take the next or succeeding examination without the payment of an additional fee. In the event a contract testing service is utilized, the fee associated with administering the test shall be collected by the testing provider and the application fee for any real estate license shall be collected by the commission.

(4) Except as provided in Section 33-1-39, it shall be the duty of all persons, partnerships, associations, companies or corporations licensed to practice as a real estate broker or salesperson to register with the commission annually or biennially, in the discretion of the commission, according to rules promulgated by it and to pay the proper registration fee. An application for renewal of license shall be made to the commission annually no later than December 31 of each year, or biennially on a date set by the commission. A licensee failing to pay his renewal fee after the same becomes due and after two (2) months' written notice of his delinquency mailed to him by United States certified mail addressed to his address of record with the commission shall thereby have his license

automatically cancelled. Any licensee renewing in this grace period shall pay a penalty in the amount of one hundred percent (100%) of the renewal fee. The renewal fee shall not exceed Seventy-five Dollars ($75.00) per year for real estate brokers, partnerships, associations and corporations. The renewal fee for a real estate salesperson's license shall not exceed Sixty Dollars ($60.00) per year.

(5) For each additional office or place of business, an annual fee not to exceed Fifty Dollars ($50.00) shall be charged.

(6) For each change of office or place of business, a fee not to exceed Fifty Dollars ($50.00) shall be charged.

(7) For each duplicate or transfer of salesperson's license, a fee not to exceed Fifty Dollars ($50.00) shall be charged.

(8) For each duplicate license, where the original license is lost or destroyed, and affidavit made thereof, a fee not to exceed Fifty Dollars ($50.00) shall be charged.

(9) To change status as a licensee from active to inactive status, a fee not to exceed Twenty-five Dollars ($25.00) shall be charged. To change status as a licensee from inactive to active status, a fee not to exceed Fifty Dollars ($50.00) shall be charged.

(10) For each bad check received by the commission, a fee not to exceed Twenty-five Dollars ($25.00) shall be charged.

(11) A fee not to exceed Five Dollars ($5.00) per hour of instruction may be charged to allay costs of seminars for educational purposes provided by the commission.

(12) A fee not to exceed Twenty-five Dollars ($25.00) may be charged for furnishing any person a copy of a real estate license, a notarized certificate of licensure or other official record of the commission.

(13) A fee not to exceed One Hundred Dollars ($100.00) shall be charged to review and process the application and instructional materials for each curriculum seeking acceptance as a real estate continuing education course developed to satisfy the mandatory continuing education requirements for this chapter, with the period of approval expiring after one (1) year. A fee not to exceed Fifty Dollars ($50.00) shall be charged for each renewal of a previously approved course, with the period of renewal expiring after one (1) year. (14) Fees, up to the limits specified herein, shall be established by the Mississippi Real Estate Commission.

§ 73-35-18. License renewal; continuing education requirements; exemptions; rules and regulations; reinstatement of expired license.

(1) Each individual applicant for renewal of a license issued by the Mississippi Real Estate Commission shall, on or before the expiration date of his license, or at a time directed by the commission, submit proof of completion of not less than sixteen (16) clock hours of approved course work to the commission, in addition to any other requirements for renewal.

The sixteen (16) clock hours' course work requirement shall apply to each two-year license renewal, and hours in excess thereof shall not be cumulated or credited for the purposes of subsequent license renewals except as provided in this subsection

(1). The commission shall develop standards for approval of courses and shall require certification of such course work of the applicant. The commission may determine any required subject matter within the mandated sixteen (16) hours; provided that the required subjects shall not exceed eight (8) hours of the total sixteen (16) hours.

Approved continuing education hours earned in the final three (3) months of a licensee's renewal period, if in excess of the required minimum sixteen (16) hours, may be carried over and credited to the next renewal period. However, no more than six (6) hours may be carried over in this manner.

Any member of the Mississippi Legislature who has a real estate license shall be credited with eight (8) hours of credit for the attendance of each year of a legislative session. No person may receive continuing education credit for prelicense education courses taken, except as follows: a licensee whose license is on inactive status and whose continuing education credits are at least thirty (30) hours in arrears may, at the discretion of the commission, receive continuing education credit for retaking prelicense coursework, provided the entire prelicense course is retaken.

(2) This section shall apply to renewals of licenses which expire on and after July 1, 1994; however, an applicant for first renewal who has been licensed for not more than one (1) year shall not be required to comply with this section for the first renewal of the applicant's license. The provisions of this section shall not apply to persons who have held a broker's or salesperson's license in this state for at least twenty-five (25) years and who are older than seventy (70) years of age. Inactive licensees are not required to meet the real estate continuing education requirements specified in this section; however, such inactive licensees, before activating their license to active status, must cumulatively meet requirements missed during the period their license was inactive.

(3) The commission shall promulgate rules and regulations as necessary to accomplish the purposes of this section in accordance with the Mississippi Administrative Procedures Law.

§ 73-35-19. Real estate license fund

All fees charged and collected under this chapter shall be paid by the administrator at least once a week, accompanied by a detailed statement thereof, into the treasury of the state to credit of a fund to be known as the "Real Estate License Fund," which fund is hereby created.

All monies which shall be paid into the State Treasury and credited to the "Real Estate License Fund" are hereby appropriated to the use of the commission in carrying out the provisions of this chapter including the payment of salaries and expenses, printing an annual directory of licensees, and for educational purposes. Maintenance of a searchable, internet-based web site shall satisfy the requirement for publication of a directory of licensees under this section.

§ 73-35-21. Grounds for refusing to issue or suspending or revoking license; hearing

(1) The commission may, upon its own motion and shall upon the verified complaint in writing of any person, hold a hearing for the refusal of license or for the suspension or revocation of a license previously issued, or for such other action as the commission deems appropriate. The commission shall have full power to refuse a license for cause or to revoke or suspend a license where it has been obtained by false or fraudulent representation, or where the licensee in performing or attempting to perform any of the acts mentioned herein, is deemed to be guilty of:

(a) Making any substantial misrepresentation in connection with a real estate transaction;

(b) Making any false promises of a character likely to influence, persuade or induce;

(c) Pursuing a continued and flagrant course of misrepresentation or making false promises through agents or salespersons or any medium of advertising or otherwise;

(d) Any misleading or untruthful advertising;

(e) Acting for more than one (1) party in a transaction or receiving compensation from more than one (1) party in a transaction, or both, without the knowledge of all parties for whom he acts;

(f) Failing, within a reasonable time, to account for or to remit any monies coming into his possession which belong to others, or commingling of monies belonging to others with his own funds. Every responsible broker procuring the execution of an earnest money contract or option or other contract who shall take or receive any cash or checks shall deposit, within a reasonable period of time, the sum or sums so received in a trust or escrow account in a bank or trust company pending the consummation or termination of the transaction. "Reasonable time" in this context means by the close of business of the next banking day;

(g) Entering a guilty plea or conviction in a court of competent jurisdiction of this state, or any other state or the United States of any felony;

(h) Displaying a "for sale" or "for rent" sign on any property without the owner's consent;

(i) Failing to furnish voluntarily, at the time of signing, copies of all listings, contracts and agreements to all parties executing the same;

(j) Paying any rebate, profit or commission to any person other than a real estate broker or salesperson licensed under the provisions of this chapter;

(k) Inducing any party to a contract, sale or lease to break such contract for the purpose of substituting in lieu thereof a new contract, where such substitution is motivated by the personal gain of the licensee;

(*l*) Accepting a commission or valuable consideration as a real estate salesperson for the performance of any of the acts specified in this chapter from any person, except his employer who must be a licensed real estate broker; or

(m) Failing to successfully pass the commission's background investigation for licensure or renewal as provided in Section 73-35-10; or

43

(n) Any act or conduct, whether of the same or a different character than hereinabove specified, which constitutes or demonstrates bad faith, incompetency or untrustworthiness, or dishonest, fraudulent or improper dealing. However, simple contact and/or communication with any mortgage broker or lender by a real estate licensee about any professional, including, but not limited to, an appraiser, home inspector, contractor, and/or attorney regarding a listing and/or a prospective or pending contract for the lease, sale and/or purchase of real estate shall not constitute conduct in violation of this section.

(2) No real estate broker shall practice law or give legal advice directly or indirectly unless said broker be a duly licensed attorney under the laws of this state. He shall not act as a public conveyancer nor give advice or opinions as to the legal effect of instruments nor give opinions concerning the validity of title to real estate; nor shall he prevent or discourage any party to a real estate transaction from employing the services of an attorney; nor shall a broker undertake to prepare documents fixing and defining the legal rights of parties to a transaction. However, when acting as a broker, he may use an earnest money contract form. A real estate broker shall not participate in attorney's fees, unless the broker is a duly licensed attorney under the laws of this state and performs legal services in addition to brokerage services.

(3) It is expressly provided that it is not the intent and purpose of the Mississippi Legislature to prevent a license from being issued to any person who is found to be of good reputation, is able to give bond, and who has lived in the State of Mississippi for the required period or is otherwise qualified under this chapter.

(4) In addition to the reasons specified in subsection (1) of this section, the commission shall be authorized to suspend the license of any licensee for being out of compliance with an order for support, as defined in Section 93-11-153.

The procedure for suspension of a license for being out of compliance with an order for support, and the procedure for the reissuance or reinstatement of a license suspended for that purpose, and the payment of any fees for the reissuance or reinstatement of a license suspended for that purpose, shall be governed by Section 93-11-157 or 93-11-163, as the case may be. If there is any conflict between any provision of Section 93-11-157 or 93-11-163 and any provision of this chapter, the provisions of Section 93-11-157 or 93-11-163, as the case may be, shall control.

(5) Nothing in this chapter shall prevent an associate broker or salesperson from owning any lawfully constituted business organization, including, but not limited to, a corporation, limited liability company or limited liability partnership, for the purpose of receiving payments contemplated in this chapter. The business organization shall not be required to be licensed under this chapter and shall not engage in any other activity requiring a real estate license.

§ 73-35-23. Powers of commission as to violations; hearings upon revocation; subpoena

(1) The commission is hereby authorized and directed to take legal action against any violator of this chapter. Upon complaint initiated by the commission or filed with it, the licensee or any Rev. 10/2016

other person charged with a violation of this chapter shall be given fifteen (15) days' notice of the hearing upon the charges filed, together with a copy of the complaint. The applicant or licensee or other violator shall have an opportunity to be heard in person or by counsel, to offer testimony, and to examine witnesses appearing in connection with the complaint.

Hearings shall be held at the offices of the Mississippi Real Estate Commission, or at the commission's sole discretion, at a place determined by the commission. At such hearings, all witnesses shall be sworn and stenographic notes of the proceedings shall be taken and filed as a part of the record in the case.

Any party to the proceedings shall be furnished with a copy of such stenographic notes upon payment to the commission of such fees as it shall prescribe, not exceeding, however, the actual cost to the commission. The commission shall render a decision on any complaint and shall immediately notify the parties to the proceedings in writing of its ruling, order or decision.

(2) In addition to the authority granted to the commission as hereinabove set forth, the commission is hereby vested with the authority to bring injunctive proceedings in any appropriate forum against any violator or violators of this chapter, and all judges or courts now having the power to grant injunctions are specifically granted the power and jurisdiction to hear and dispose of such proceedings.

(3) The commission is hereby authorized and empowered to issue subpoenas for the attendance of witnesses and the production of books and papers. The process issued by the commission shall extend to all parts of the state, and such process shall be served by any person designated by the commission for such service. The person serving such process receive such compensation as may be allowed by the commission, not to exceed the fee prescribed by law for similar services. All witnesses who are subpoenaed and who appear in any proceedings before the commission receive the same fees and mileage as allowed by law, and all such fees shall be taxed as part of the costs in the case.

(4) Where in any proceeding before the commission any witness shall fail or refuse to attend upon subpoena issued by the commission, shall refuse to testify, or shall refuse to produce any books and papers the production of which is called for by the subpoena, the attendance of such witness and the giving of his testimony and the production of the books and papers shall be enforced by any court of competent jurisdiction of this state in the same manner as the attendance and testimony of witnesses in civil cases are enforced in the courts of this state.

(5) The commission may obtain legal counsel privately to represent it in proceedings when legal counsel is required.

§ 73-35-25. Appeals

(1) Any applicant or licensee or person aggrieved shall have the right of appeal from any adverse ruling or order or decision of the commission to the circuit court of the county of residence of the applicant, licensee or person, or of the First Judicial District of Hinds County, within thirty (30) days from the service of notice of the action of the commission upon the parties in interest.

(2) Notice of appeals shall be filed in the office of the clerk of the court who shall issue a writ of certiorari directed to the commission commanding it, within thirty (30) days after service thereof, to certify to such court its entire record in the matter in which the appeal has been taken. The appeal shall thereupon be heard in due course by said court, without a jury, which shall review the record and make its determination of the cause between the parties.

(3) Any order, rule or decision of the commission shall not take effect until after the time for appeal to said court shall have expired. In the event an appeal is taken by a defendant, such appeal may act, in the discretion of the court, as a supersedeas and the court shall dispose of said appeal and enter its decision promptly.

(4) Any person taking an appeal shall post a satisfactory bond in the amount of Five Hundred Dollars ($500.00) for the payment of any costs which may be adjudged against him.

(5) Actions taken by the commission in suspending a license when required by Section 93-11-157 or 93-11-163 are not actions from which an appeal may be taken under this section. Any appeal of a license suspension that is required by Section 93-11-157 or 93-11-163 shall be taken in accordance with the appeal procedure specified in Section 93-11-157 or 93-11-163, as the case may be, rather than the procedure specified in this section.

§ 73-35-27. Duties of commission

(1) The commission is hereby authorized to assist in conducting or holding real estate courses or institutes, and to incur and pay the necessary expenses in connection therewith, which courses or institutes shall be open to any licensee or other interested parties.

(2) The commission is hereby authorized to assist libraries, real estate institutes, and foundations with financial aid, or otherwise, in providing texts, sponsoring studies, surveys and educational programs for the benefit of real estate and the elevation of the real estate business.

§ 73-35-29. Administrator to give bond

The administrator, appointed by the commission, in the discretion of the commission, shall give bond in such sum and with such surety as the commission may direct and approve, and the premium thereon shall be paid by the commission.

§ 73-35-31. Penalties for violations of chapter

(1) Any person violating a provision of this chapter shall, upon conviction of a first violation thereof, if a person, be punished by a fine or not less than Five Hundred Dollars ($500.00) nor more than One Thousand Dollars ($1,000.00), or by imprisonment for a term not to exceed ninety (90) days, or both; and if a corporation, be punished by a fine of not more than Two Thousand Dollars ($2,000.00). Upon conviction of a second or subsequent violation, if a person, shall be punished by a fine of not less than One Thousand Dollars ($1,000.00) nor more than Two Thousand Dollars ($2,000.00), or by imprisonment for a term not to exceed six (6) months, or both; and if a corporation, be punished by a fine of not less than Two Thousand Dollars ($2,000.00) nor more than Five Thousand Dollars ($5,000.00).

Any officer or agent of a corporation, or any member or agent of a partnership or association, who shall personally participate in or be accessory to any violation of this chapter by such corporation, partnership or association, shall be subject to the penalties herein prescribed for individuals.

(2) In case any person, partnership, association or corporation shall have received any sum of money, or the equivalent thereto, as commission, compensation or profit by or in consequence of his violation of any provision of this chapter, such person, partnership, association or corporation shall also be liable to a penalty of not less than the amount of the sum of money so received and not more than four (4) times the sum so received, as may be determined by the court, which penalty may be sued for and recovered by any person aggrieved and for his use and benefit, in any court of competent jurisdiction.

(3) No fee, commission or other valuable consideration may be paid to a person for real estate brokerage activities as described in subsection (1) of Section 73-35-3 unless the person provides evidence of licensure under the provisions of this chapter or provides evidence of a cooperative agreement provided under the authority of Section 73-35-11.

§ 73-35-33. License required to sue for compensation; suit by salesperson in own name

(1) No person, partnership, association or corporation shall bring or maintain an action in any court of this state for the recovery of a commission, fee or compensation for any act done or services rendered, the doing or rendering of which is prohibited under the provisions of this chapter for persons other than licensed real estate brokers, unless such person was duly licensed hereunder as a real estate broker at the time of the doing of such act or the rendering of such service.

(2) No real estate salesperson shall have the right to institute suits in his own name for the recovery of a fee, commission or compensation for services as a real estate salesperson, but any such action shall be instituted and brought by the broker employing such salesperson. However, any real estate salesperson shall have the right to bring an action in his own name if the action is against the

broker employing such salesperson for the recovery of any fees owed to him.

§ 73-35-35. Commission to adopt rules and regulations

The commission may act by a majority of the members thereof, and authority is hereby given to the commission to adopt, fix and establish all rules and regulations in its opinion necessary for the conduct of its business, the holdings of hearings before it, and otherwise generally for the enforcement and administration of the provisions of this chapter. Further, the commission is empowered with the authority to adopt such rules and regulations as it deems appropriate to regulate the sale of timesharing and condominium properties within the state of Mississippi and the sale of timesharing and condominium properties in other states to residents of Mississippi.

§ 73-35-101. Short title

Sections 73-35-101 through 73-35-105 shall be known and may be cited as the "Interest on Real Estate Brokers' Escrow Accounts Act."

§ 73-35-103. Definitions

As used in Sections 73-35-101 through 73-35-105, the following terms shall have the meanings ascribed herein unless the context clearly indicates otherwise:

(a) "Real estate broker" or "broker" means an individual, partnership or corporation licensed pursuant to Section 73-35-1 et seq., and as defined under Section 73-35-3(1).

(b) "IREBEA" means the program created and governed by Sections 73-35-101 through 73-35-105.

(c) "Interest earnings" means the total interest earnings generated by the IREBEA at each individual financial institution.

(d) "Local affiliate of Habitat for Humanity International, Inc.," means an independently run 501(c)(3) organization that acts in partnership with and on behalf of Habitat for Humanity International, Inc., to coordinate all aspects of Habitat home building in a specific geographical area.

(e) Local affiliate of Fuller Center for Housing, Inc., means an independently run 501(c)(3) organization that acts in partnership with and on behalf of Fuller Center for Housing, Inc., to coordinate all aspects of home building on behalf of the Fuller Center in a specific geographical area.

(f) "Chair of real estate" means the endowment fund held and administered by any Mississippi university. For those universities which do not designate or which do not have a "chair of real estate," the term "chair of real estate" includes a professorship of real estate.

§ 73-35-105. Interest on Real Estate Brokers' Escrow Accounts (IREBEA) program

(1) The IREBEA program shall be a voluntary program based upon willing participation by real estate brokers, whether proprietorships, partnerships or professional corporations. (2) IREBEA shall apply to all clients or customers of the participating brokers whose funds on deposit are either nominal in amount or to be held for a short period of time. (3) The following principles shall apply to clients' or customers' funds which are held by brokers who elect to participate in IREBEA: (a) No earnings on the IREBEA accounts may be made available to or utilized by a broker.

(b) Upon the request of the client or customer, earnings may be made available to the client whenever possible upon deposited funds which are neither nominal in amount nor to be held for a short period of time; however, traditional broker-client or broker-customer relationships do not compel brokers either to invest clients' or customers' funds or to advise clients or customers to make their funds productive.

(c) Clients' or customers' funds which are nominal in amount or to be held for a short period of time shall be retained in an interest-bearing checking or savings trust account with the interest, less any service charge or fees, made payable at least quarterly to any chair of real estate, local affiliate of Habitat for Humanity International, Inc., or local affiliate of Fuller Center for Housing, Inc. A separate accounting shall be made annually for all funds received.

(d) The broker shall select in writing that the chair of real estate, local affiliate of Habitat for Humanity International, Inc., or local affiliate of Fuller Center for Housing, Inc., shall be the beneficiary of such funds for the interest earnings on such funds. The interest earnings shall not be divided between one or more beneficiaries.

(e) The determination of whether clients' or customers' funds are nominal in amount or to be held for a short period of time rests in the sound judgment of each broker, and no charge of ethical impropriety or other breach of professional conduct shall attend a broker's exercise of judgment in that regard.

(f) Notification to clients or customers whose funds are nominal in amount or to be held for a short period of time is unnecessary for those brokers who choose to participate in the program. Participation in the IREBEA program is accomplished by the broker's written notification to an authorized financial institution. That communication shall contain an expression of the broker's desire to participate in the program and, if the institution has not already received appropriate notification, advice regarding the Internal Revenue Service's approval of the taxability of earned interest or dividends to a chair of real estate, or a local affiliate of Habitat for Humanity International, Inc., or local affiliate of Fuller Center for Housing, Inc.

(4) The following principles shall apply to those clients' or customers' funds held in trust accounts by brokers who elect not to participate in IREBEA:

(a) No earnings from the funds may be made available to any broker.

(b) Upon the request of a client or customer, earnings may be made available to the client or customer whenever possible upon deposited funds which are neither nominal in amount nor to be held for a short period of time; however, traditional broker-client or broker-customer relationships do not compel brokers either to invest clients' or customers' funds or to advise clients or customers to make their funds productive.

(c) Clients' or customers' funds which are nominal in amount or to be held for short periods of time, and for which individual income generation allocation is not arranged with a financial institution, shall be retained in a noninterest-bearing demand trust account.

(d) The determination of whether clients' or customers' funds are nominal in amount or to be held for a short period of time rests in the sound judgment of each broker, and no charge of ethical impropriety or other breach of professional conduct shall attend a broker's exercise of judgment in that regard.

(5) The Mississippi Real Estate Commission shall adopt appropriate and necessary rules in compliance with the provisions of Sections 73-35-101 through 73-35-105.

§ 89-1-501. Applicability of real estate transfer disclosure requirement provisions

(1) The provisions of Sections 89-1-501 through 89-1-523 apply only with respect to transfers by sale, exchange, installment land sale contract, lease with an option to purchase, any other option to purchase or ground lease coupled with improvements, of real property on which a dwelling unit is located, or residential stock cooperative improved with or consisting of not less than one (1) nor more than four (4) dwelling units, when the execution of such

transfers is by, or with the aid of, a duly licensed real estate broker or salesperson.

(2) There are specifically excluded from the provisions of Sections 89-1-501 through 89-1-523:

(a) Transfers pursuant to court order, including, but not limited to, transfers ordered by a probate court in administration of an estate, transfers pursuant to a writ of execution, transfers by any foreclosure sale, transfers by a trustee in bankruptcy, transfers by eminent domain, and transfers resulting from a decree for specific performance.

(b) Transfers to a mortgagee by a mortgagor or successor in interest who is in default, transfers to a beneficiary of a deed of trust by a trustor or successor in interest who is in default, transfers by any foreclosure sale after default, in an obligation secured by a mortgage, transfers by a sale under a power of sale or any foreclosure sale under a decree of foreclosure after default in an obligation secured by a deed of trust or secured by any other instrument containing a power of sale, or transfers by a mortgagee or a beneficiary under a deed of trust who has acquired the real property at a sale conducted pursuant to a power of sale under a mortgage or deed of trust or a sale pursuant to a decree of foreclosure or has acquired the real property by a deed in lieu of foreclosure.

(c) Transfers by a fiduciary in the course of the administration of a decedent's estate, guardianship, conservatorship or trust.

(d) Transfers from one co-owner to one or more other co-owners.

(e) Transfers made to a spouse, or to a person or persons in the lineal line of consanguinity of one or more of the transferors.

(f) Transfers between spouses resulting from a decree of dissolution of marriage or a decree of legal separation or from a property settlement agreement incidental to such a decree.

(g) Transfers or exchanges to or from any governmental entity. Rev. 10/2016

(h) Transfers of real property on which no dwelling is located. (i) The provisions of Section 89-1-527.

§ 89-1-503. Delivery of written statement required; indication of compliance; right of transferee to terminate for late delivery

The transferor of any real property subject to Sections 89-1-501 through 89-1-523 shall deliver to the prospective transferee the written property condition disclosure statement required by Sections 89-1-501 through 89-1-523, as follows:

(a) In the case of a sale, as soon as practicable before transfer of title.

(b) In the case of transfer by a real property sales contract, or by a lease together with an option to purchase, or a ground lease coupled with improvements, as soon as practicable before execution of the contract. For the purpose of this paragraph, execution means the making or acceptance of an offer. With respect to any transfer subject to paragraph (a) or (b), the transferor shall indicate compliance with Sections 89-1-501 through 89-1-523 either on the receipt for deposit, the real property sales contract, the lease, or any addendum attached thereto or on a separate document. If any disclosure, or any material amendment of any disclosure, required to be made by Section 89-1-501 through 89-1-523, is delivered after the execution of an offer to purchase, the transferee shall have three (3) days after delivery in person or five (5) days after delivery by deposit in the mail, to terminate his or her offer by delivery of a written notice of termination to the transferor or the transferor's agent.

§ 89-1-505. Limit on duties and liabilities with respect to information required or delivered

(1) Neither the transferor nor any listing or selling agent shall be liable for any error, inaccuracy or omission of any information delivered pursuant to Sections 89-1-501 through 89-1-523 if the error, inaccuracy or omission was not within the personal knowledge of the transferor or that listing or selling agent, was based on information timely provided by public agencies or by other persons providing information as specified in subsection (2) that is required to be disclosed pursuant to Sections 89-1-501 through 89-1-523, and ordinary care was exercised in obtaining and transmitting it.

(2) The delivery of any information required to be disclosed by Sections 89-1-501 through 89-1-523 to a prospective transferee by a public agency or other person providing information required to be disclosed pursuant to Sections 89-1-501 through 89-1-523 shall be deemed to comply with the requirements of Sections 89-1-501 through 89-1-523 and shall relieve the transferor or any listing or selling agent of any further duty under Sections 89-1-501 through 89-1-523 with respect to that item of information. Rev. 10/2016

(3) The delivery of a report or opinion prepared by a licensed engineer, land surveyor, geologist, structural pest control operator, contractor or other expert, dealing with matters within the scope of the professional's license or expertise, shall be sufficient compliance for application of the exemption provided by subsection (1) if the information is provided to the prospective transferee pursuant to a request therefor, whether written or oral. In responding to such a request, an expert may indicate, in writing, an understanding that the information provided will be used in fulfilling the requirements of Section 89-1-509 and, if so, shall indicate the required disclosures, or parts thereof, to which the information being furnished is applicable. Where such a statement is furnished, the expert shall not be responsible for any items of information, or parts thereof, other than those expressly set forth in the statement.

§ 89-1-507. Approximation of certain information required to be disclosed; information subsequently rendered inaccurate

If information disclosed in accordance with Sections 89-1-501 through 89-1-523 is subsequently rendered inaccurate as a result of any act, occurrence or agreement subsequent to the delivery of the required disclosures, the inaccuracy resulting therefrom does not constitute a violation of Sections 89-1-501 through 89-1-523. If at the time the disclosures are required to be made, an item of information required to be disclosed is unknown or not available to the transferor, and the transferor or his agent has made a reasonable effort to ascertain it, the transferor may use an approximation of the information, provided the approximation is clearly identified as such, is reasonable, is based on the best information available to the transferor or his agent, and is not used for the purpose of circumventing or evading Sections 89-1-501 through 89-1-523.

§ 89-1-509. Form of seller's disclosure statement

The disclosures required by Sections 89-1-501 through 89-1-523 pertaining to the property proposed to be transferred shall be set forth in, and shall be made on a copy of a disclosure form, the structure and composition of which shall be determined by the Mississippi Real Estate Commission.

§ 89-1-511. Disclosures to be made in good faith

Each disclosure required by Sections 89-1-501 through 89-1-523 and each act which may be performed in making the disclosure, shall be made in good faith. For purposes of Sections 89-1-501 through 89-1-523, "good faith" means honesty in fact in the conduct of the transaction.

§ 89-1-513. Provisions not exhaustive of items to be disclosed

The specification of items for disclosure in Sections 89-1-501 through 89-1-523 does not limit or abridge any obligation for disclosure created by any other provision of law or which may exist in order to avoid fraud, misrepresentation or deceit in the transfer transaction.

§ 89-1-515. Amendment of disclosure

Any disclosure made pursuant to Sections 89-1-501 through 89-1-523 may be amended in writing by the transferor or his agent, but the amendment shall be subject to the provisions of Section 89-1-503.

§ 89-1-517. Delivery of disclosure

Delivery of disclosure required by Sections 89-1-501 through 89-1-523 shall be by personal delivery to the transferee or by mail to the prospective transferee. For the purposes of Sections 89-1-501 through 89-1-523, delivery to the spouse of a transferee shall be deemed delivery to the transferee, unless provided otherwise by contract.

§ 89-1-519. Agent; extent of agency

Any person or entity, other than a duly licensed real estate broker or salesperson acting in the capacity of an escrow agent for the transfer of real property subject to Sections 89-1-501 through 89-1-523 shall not be deemed the agent of the transferor or transferee for purposes of the disclosure requirements of Sections 89-1-501 through 89-1-523, unless the person or entity is empowered to so act by an express written agreement to that effect. The extent of such an agency shall be governed by the written agreement.

§ 89-1-521. Delivery of disclosure where more than one agent; inability of delivering broker to obtain disclosure document; notification to transferee of right to disclosure

(1) If more than one (1) licensed real estate broker is acting as an agent in a transaction subject to Sections 89-1-501 through 89-1-523, the broker who has obtained the offer made by the transferee shall, except as otherwise provided in Sections 89-1-501 through 89-1-523, deliver the disclosure required by Sections 89-1-501 through 89-1-523 to the transferee, unless the transferor has given other written instructions for delivery.

(2) If a licensed real estate broker responsible for delivering the disclosures under this section cannot obtain the disclosure document required and does not have written assurance from the transferee that the disclosure has been received, the broker shall advise the transferee in writing of his rights to the disclosure. A licensed real estate broker responsible for delivering disclosures under this section shall maintain a record of the action taken to effect compliance.

§ 89-1-523. Noncompliance with disclosure requirements not to invalidate transfer; liability for actual damages

No transfer subject to Sections 89-1-501 through 89-1-523 shall be invalidated solely because of the failure of any person to comply with any provision of Sections 89-1-501 through 89-1-523. However, any person who willfully or negligently violates or fails to perform any duty prescribed by any provision of Sections 89-1-501 through 89-1-523 shall be liable in the amount of actual damages suffered by a transferee.

§ 89-1-525. Enforcement by Mississippi Real Estate Commission

The Mississippi Real Estate Commission is authorized to enforce the provisions of Sections 89-1-501 through 89-1-523. Any violation of the provisions of Sections 89-1-501 through 89-1-523 shall be treated in the same manner as a violation of the Real Estate Broker License Law of 1954, Section 73-35-1 et seq., and shall be subject to same penalties as provided in that chapter.

§ 89-1-527. Failure to disclose nonmaterial fact regarding property as site of death or felony crime, as site of act or occurrence having no effect on physical condition of property, or as being owned or occupied by persons affected or exposed to certain diseases; failure to disclose information provided or maintained on registration of sex offenders

(1) The fact or suspicion that real property is or was:

(a) The site of a natural death, suicide, homicide or felony crime (except for illegal drug activity that affects the physical condition of the property, its physical environment or the improvements located thereon);

(b) The site of an act or occurrence that had no effect on the physical condition of the property, its physical environment or the improvements located thereon;

(c) Owned or occupied by a person affected or exposed to any disease not known to be transmitted through common occupancy of real estate including, but not limited to, the human immunodeficiency virus (HIV) and the acquired immune deficiency syndrome (AIDS); does not constitute a material fact that must be disclosed in a real estate transaction. A failure to disclose such nonmaterial facts or suspicions shall not give rise to a criminal, civil or administrative action against the owner of such real property, a licensed real estate broker or any affiliated licensee of the broker.

(2) A failure to disclose in any real estate transaction any information that is provided or maintained, or is required to be provided or maintained, in accordance with Section 45-33-21 through Section 45-33-57, shall not give rise to a cause of action against an owner of real property, a licensed real estate broker or any affiliated licensee of the broker. Likewise, no cause of action shall arise against any licensed real estate broker or affiliated licensee of the broker for revealing information to a seller or buyer of real estate in accordance with Section 45-33-21 through Section 45-33-57. Any factors related to this paragraph, if known to a property owner or licensee shall be disclosed if requested by a consumer.

(3) Failure to disclose any of the facts or suspicions of facts described in subsections (1) and (2) shall not be grounds for the termination or rescission of any transaction in which real property has been or will be transferred or leased. This provision does not preclude an action against an owner of real estate who makes

intentional or fraudulent misrepresentations in response to a direct inquiry from a purchaser or prospective purchaser regarding facts or suspicions that are not material to the physical condition of the property including, but not limited to, those factors listed in subsections (1) and (2).

Mississippi Real Estate Commission

Mississippi Real Estate Commission Rules and Regulations

TITLE 30: Professions and Occupations

PART 1601: Mississippi Real Estate Commission

Part 1601 Chapter 1: Licensing

Rule 1.1 Applying for a License

A. An applicant for a broker's license must pass the National Portion of the broker's examination with a grade of at least 75% and must pass the State Specific Portion of the examination with a grade of at least 80%.

B. An applicant for a salesperson's license must pass the National Portion of the salesperson's examination with a grade of at least 70% and must pass the State Specific Portion of the examination with a grade of at least 75%.

C. An application fee must accompany the application and will not be refunded after the applicant is scheduled for the examination.

D. The approved Examination Testing Provider will administer examination in various locations in and near the State of Mississippi. Applicants will arrange the time and place of their examination with the Testing Provider.

E. When an applicant is approved for either examination, applicant has two months in which to take and pass both the National Portion and the State Specific Portion of the examination. If the applicant fails to appear for the examination within the two months allowed, applicant's fee will be forfeited and their file closed. If the applicant fails to pass the first examination, applicant will be allowed to take the next examination with the payment of an additional fee to the Testing Provider. If the applicant fails to appear for the second examination, fees will be forfeited and their file closed.

F. If a corporation has been chartered by the state of Mississippi, the license will be issued in the corporate name except that no license will be issued for a corporation, company, or trade name where there exists in that county or trade area a real estate broker or real estate agency having a substantially similar name.

G. A real estate licensee of another state who desires to obtain a license under this chapter shall be exempt from the examination provided the examination administered in the other state is determined by the Commission to be equivalent to such examination given in this state and provided that such other state extends this same privilege or exemption to Mississippi real estate licensees.

Real estate education courses obtained through sources (providers) other than those set forth in Section 73-35-7 of the statute but which are accepted in the state where the applicant is licensed, may be accepted by the Commission provided the state where the applicant is licensed has entered into a reciprocal agreement with this state.

Source: Miss. Code Ann. §§ 73-35-35

Rule 1.2 Changing the Status of a License

A. To change a license from active to inactive status, licensee shall notify the Commission in writing, shall insure that the license is returned to the Commission and shall pay the appropriate fee. A licensee who is on inactive status at time of renewal may renew the license on inactive status by filing a renewal application and paying the renewal fee. A broker who terminates a real estate business may place the business license on inactive status. To return to active status, a salesperson or broker/salesperson must file a transfer application. A broker and/or a business license may be activated by notifying the Commission by letter or transfer application including required fee.

B. When a licensee wishes to transfer from one broker to another, the transferring licensee must file a transfer application signed by the new broker accompanied by the transfer fee and must furnish a statement that the licensee is not carrying any listings or pertinent information belonging to the former broker unless that broker so consents.

C. Any licensee who has entered active duty military service due to draft laws or national emergency shall, upon his return to civilian life and within twelve (12) months after honorable discharge, be considered, so far as this Commission is concerned, to have been continuously engaged in the real estate business in the same capacity as when the licensee entered military service.

Source: Miss. Code Ann. §§ 73-35-35

Part 1601 Chapter 2: Fees

Rule 2.1

The following fees are set by the Commission in accordance with Section 73-35-17:

A. Application and one year's use of license:

(1) Broker... $150.00

(2) Salesperson... $120.00

B. Application for license as a real estate broker issued for partnership, association, or corporation and one year's use of license:

(1) Partnership, association or corporation................... $ 75.00

(2) Branch Office..$ 50.00

C. Renewal fees for two-year period (Maximum):

(1) Broker (individual)... $150.00

(2) Broker (partnership, association, corporation)...... ... $150.00

(3) Salesperson... $120.00

(4) Branch Office... $100.00

Penalty for late renewal within grace period - 100%

D. Changes:

(1) Place of business change (active license only)......... $ 50.00

(2) Each duplicate license.................................... $ 50.00

(3) Each transfer of license.................................... $ 50.00

(4) Status change from active to inactive status............ $ 25.00

(5) Status change from inactive to active status............ $ 50.00

E. Check charge:

(1) Each check returned not paid to the Commission......$ 25.00

Source: Miss. Code Ann. §§ 73-35-35

Rule 2.2 All fees are the same for both Resident and Nonresident Licenses.

Fees and monies payable to the Mississippi Real Estate

Commission may be by personal check, cash, cashier's check or money order. All personal checks shall be made payable to the Mississippi Real Estate Commission. Any personal checks returned not paid or for any other reason shall constitute justifiable grounds for refusing, suspending or revoking a license.

Non-sufficient fund (NSF) checks, if not made good by renewal deadline, will cause the licensee to be in non-renewal status and necessitates the payment of a penalty (100%) by licensee.

Source: Miss. Code Ann. §§ 73-35-35

Part 1601 Chapter 3: Administration/Conducting Business

Rule 3.1 General Rules

A. It shall be the duty of the responsible broker to instruct the licensees licensed under that 4

broker in the fundamentals of real estate practice, ethics of the profession and the Mississippi Real Estate License Law and to exercise supervision of their real estate activities for which a license is required.

B. A real estate broker who operates under the supervision of a responsible broker must not at any time act independently as a broker. The responsible broker shall at all times be responsible for the action of the affiliated broker to the same extent as though that licensee were a salesperson and that affiliated broker shall not perform any real estate service without the full consent and knowledge of his employing or supervising broker.

However, should the responsible broker agree that a broker under his supervision may perform certain real estate services outside the responsible broker's supervision or direction, the responsible broker shall notify the Commission in writing as to the exact nature of such relationship and the names of the broker or brokers involved. The responsible broker shall immediately notify the Commission in writing upon the termination of such relationship.

C. A licensed Mississippi broker may cooperate with a broker licensed in another state who does not hold a Mississippi license through the use of a cooperative agreement. A separate cooperative agreement must be filed for each property, prospective user or transaction with said writing reflecting the compensation to be paid to the Mississippi licensed broker. The listing or property management agreement for the Mississippi real property shall in such cases remain in the name of the Mississippi licensed broker.

The commissions or other compensation resulting from the sale/rent/lease/property management or auction of the Mississippi real property and which are earned during the period the cooperative agreement is in force shall be divided on a negotiable basis between the Mississippi broker and the nonresident broker.

A responsible (principal) nonresident broker described herein is defined as an active, licensed responsible real estate broker of another state who does not possess an active responsible nonresident real estate broker's license issued by the Mississippi Real Estate Commission (MREC). A Mississippi broker described herein is a responsible (principal) real estate broker whose license is on active status and whose license was issued by MREC either as a responsible resident Mississippi broker or as a responsible nonresident Mississippi broker.

The responsible nonresident broker cannot place any sign on real property located in the state of Mississippi without the written consent of the cooperating responsible Mississippi broker. When the consent is obtained, the sign of the responsible Mississippi broker must be placed in a prominent place and in close proximity to the responsible nonresident broker's sign. Any licensed responsible Mississippi broker assisting or cooperating in the sale, lease, property management, rental or auction of real property within the state of Mississippi with a responsible nonresident broker who fails or refuses to list his or her name in such advertisement, or fails or refuses to cross-list such property with him or her, in writing, shall be deemed in violation of Section 73-35-11 of the Real Estate Broker's License Act, and shall be subject to a revocation or suspension of his or her license. In such instance herein where a responsible Mississippi broker enters into a cooperative agreement with a responsible nonresident broker pertaining to the sale of real property within the state of Mississippi, the responsible Mississippi broker must file two copies of the cooperating agreement with the Mississippi Real Estate Commission.

D. A responsible broker must maintain an office and display the license therein. If the broker has more than one office, the broker shall display a branch office license in each branch office. The broker is responsible for the real estate practices of those licensees.

E. No licensee shall pay any part of a fee, commission, or other compensation received by such licensee in buying, selling, exchanging, leasing, auctioning or renting any real estate except to another licensee through the licensee's responsible broker.

No licensee shall knowingly pay a commission, or other compensation to a licensed person knowing that licensee will in turn pay a portion or all of that which is received to a person who does not hold a real estate license.

A licensee who has changed to inactive status or who has transferred to another responsible broker may receive compensation from the previous responsible broker if the commission was generated from activity during the time that the licensee was under the supervision of that responsible broker.

F. Any licensee who fails in a timely manner to respond to official Mississippi Real Estate Commission written communication or who fails or neglects to abide by Mississippi Real Estate Commission's Rules and Regulations shall be deemed, prima facie, to be guilty of improper dealing.

G. A real estate broker or salesperson in the ordinary course of business may give an opinion as to the sales price of real estate for the purpose of a prospective listing or sale; however, this opinion as to the listing price or the sale price shall not be referred to as an appraisal and must be completed in compliance with Section 73-35-4 of the Real Estate Broker's License Act and must conform to the Standards established by the National Association of Broker Price Opinion Professionals (NABPOP).

H. When an offer is made on property owned by a party with whom a broker has entered into a listing agreement, such broker shall document and date the seller's personal acceptance or rejection of the offer and upon written request, shall provide a copy of such document to the person making the offer.

I. A real estate licensee shall not be exempt from disciplinary actions by the commission when selling property owned by the licensee.

Source: Miss. Code Ann. §§ 73-35-35

Rule 3.2 Documents 6

A. A real estate licensee shall **immediately (at the time of signing)** deliver a true and correct copy of any instrument to any party or parties executing the same.

B. All exclusive listing agreements shall be in writing, properly identify the property to be sold, and contain all of the terms and conditions under which the transaction is to be consummated;

including the sales price, the considerations to be paid, the signatures of all parties to the agreement, and a definite date of expiration. No listing agreement shall contain any provision requiring the listing party to notify the broker of their intention to cancel the listing after such definite expiration date. An "Exclusive Agency" listing or "Exclusive Right to Sell" listing shall clearly indicate in the listing agreement that it is such an agreement.

C. All exclusive buyer representation agreements shall be in writing and properly identify the terms and conditions under which the buyer will rely on the broker for the purchase of real estate; including the sales price, the considerations to be paid, the signatures of all parties to the agreement, and a definite date of expiration. The buyer may terminate the agreement upon fifteen (15) calendar days written notice to the buyer's exclusive agent. An Exclusive Buyer Representation agreement shall clearly indicate in the body of the document that it is such an agreement.

D. In the event that more than one written offer is made before the owner has accepted an offer, any other written offer received by the listing broker, whether from a prospective purchaser or from another licensee cooperating in a sale, shall be presented to the owner unless the listing broker has specific, written instructions from the owner to postpone the presentation of other offers. Broker should caution the seller against countering on more than one offer at the same time.

E. Every real estate contact must reflect whom the broker represents by a statement over the signatures of the parties to the contract.

F. No licensee shall represent to a lender or any other interested party, either verbally or through the preparation of a false sales contract, an amount in excess of the true and actual selling price.

G. A real estate broker must keep on file for three years following its consummation, complete records relating to any real estate transaction. This includes, but is not limited to: listings, options, leases, offers to purchase, contracts of sale, escrow records, agency agreements and copies of all closing statements.

Source: Miss. Code Ann. §§ 73-35-35

Rule 3.3 Advertising

A. The use of any copyrighted term or insignia on stationery, office signs, or in advertising by any licensee not authorized to do so, will be considered as "substantial misrepresentation" and cause for refusal, suspension, or revocation of the license.

A licensee shall not advertise to sell, buy, exchange, auction, rent or lease property in a manner indicating that the offer to sell, buy, exchange, auction, rent, or lease such property is being made by a private party not engaged in the real estate business. No advertisement shall be inserted by a licensee in any publication where only a post office box number, telephone number, or street address appears. Every licensee, when advertising real estate in any publication, shall indicate that the party advertising is licensed in real estate. All advertising must be under the direct supervision and in the name of the responsible broker or in the name of the real estate firm.

B. When a licensee is advertising their own property for sale, purchase or exchange which is not listed with a broker, the licensee must indicate that he or she is licensed. The disclosure of licensee's status must be made in all forms of advertising, including the "for sale" sign.

C. In addition to disclosing their licensed status in advertisements, licensees are required to disclose their licensed status on all contracts for real estate in which they have an ownership interest.

A broker shall advertise in the name in which the license is issued. A broker may use a descriptive term after the broker's name to indicate the occupation in which engaged, for example, "realty", "real estate", "property management". If advertising in any other form, a partnership, trade name, association, company or corporation license must be obtained prior to advertising in that manner.

Source: Miss. Code Ann. §§ 73-35-35

Rule 3.4 Earnest Money

A. The responsible broker is responsible at all times for earnest money deposits. Earnest money accepted by the broker or any licensee for which the broker is responsible and upon acceptance of a mutually agreeable contract is required to deposit the money into a trust account prior to the close of business of the next banking day. The responsible broker is required to promptly account for and remit the full amount of the deposit or earnest money at the consummation or termination of transaction. A licensee is required to pay over to the responsible broker all deposits and earnest money immediately upon receipt thereof. Earnest money must be returned promptly when the purchaser is rightfully entitled to same allowing reasonable time for clearance of the earnest money check. In the event of uncertainty as to the proper disposition of earnest money, the broker may turn earnest money over to a court of law for disposition. Failure to comply with this regulation shall constitute grounds for revocation or suspension of license.

B. When the broker is the agent for the seller and for any reason the seller fails or is unable to consummate the transaction, the broker has no right to any portion of the earnest money deposited by the purchaser, even if a commission has been earned. The entire amount of the earnest money deposit must be returned to the purchaser and the broker should look to the seller for compensation.

C. Accurate records shall be kept on escrow accounts of all monies received, disbursed, or on hand. All monies shall be individually identified as to a particular transaction. Escrow records shall be kept in accordance with standard accounting practices and shall be subject to inspection at all times by the Commission.

Monies received in a trust account on behalf of clients or customers are not assets of the broker; however, a broker may deposit and keep in each escrow account or rental account some personal funds for the express purpose of covering service charges and other bank debits related to each account.

D. If a broker, as escrow agent, accepts a check and later finds that such check has not been honored by the bank on which it was drawn, the broker shall immediately notify all parties involved in the transaction.

Source: Miss. Code Ann. §§ 73-35-35

Part 1601 Chapter 4: Agency Relationship Disclosure

Rule 4.1 Purpose

Consumers shall be fully informed of the agency relationships in real estate transactions identified in Section 73-35-3. This rule places specific requirements on Brokers to disclose their agency relationship. This does not abrogate the laws of agency as recognized under common law and compliance with the prescribed disclosures will not always guarantee that a Broker has fulfilled all of his responsibilities under the common law of agency. Compliance will be necessary in order to protect licensees from impositions of sanctions against their license by the Mississippi Real Estate Commission. Special situations, where unusual facts exist or where one or more parties involved are especially vulnerable, could require additional disclosures not contemplated by this rule. In such cases, Brokers should seek legal advice prior to entering into an agency relationship.

Source: Miss. Code Ann. §§ 73-35-3

Rule 4.2 Definitions

A. "Agency" shall mean the relationship created when one person, the Principal (client), delegates to another, the agent, the right to act on his behalf in a real estate transaction and to exercise some degree of discretion while so acting. Agency may be entered into by expressed agreement, implied through the actions of the agent and or ratified after the fact by the principal accepting the benefits of an agent's previously unauthorized act. An agency gives rise to a fiduciary relationship and imposes on the agent, as the fiduciary of the principal, certain duties, obligations, and high standards of good faith and loyalty.

B. "Agent" shall mean one who is authorized to act on behalf of and represent another. A real estate broker is the agent of the principal (client) to whom a fiduciary obligation is owed. Salespersons licensed under the broker are subagents of the Broker, regardless of the location of the office in which the salesperson works.

C. "Client" shall mean the person to whom the agent owes a fiduciary duty. It can be a seller, buyer, landlord, tenant or both.

D. "Compensation" is that fee paid to a broker for the rendering of services. Compensation, when considered alone, is not the determining factor in an agency relationship. The relationship can be created regardless of whether the seller pays the fee, the buyer pays the fee, both pay the fee or neither pays a fee.

E. "Customer" shall mean that person not represented in a real estate transaction. It may be the buyer, seller, landlord or tenant.

F. "Disclosed Dual Agent" shall mean that agent representing both parties to a real estate transaction with the informed consent of both parties, with written understanding of specific duties and representation to be afforded each party. There may be situations where disclosed dual agency presents conflicts of interest that cannot be resolved without breach of duty to one party or another. Brokers who practice disclosed dual agency should do so with the utmost caution to protect consumers and themselves from inadvertent violation of demanding common law standards of disclosed dual agency.

G. "Fiduciary Responsibilities" are those duties due the principal (client) in a real estate transaction are:

(1) 'Loyalty' - the agent must put the interests of the principal above the interests of the agent or any third party.

(2) 'Obedience' - the agent agrees to obey any lawful instruction from the principal in the execution of the transaction that is the subject of the agency.

(3) 'Disclosure' - the agent must disclose to the principal any information the agent becomes aware of in connection with the agency.

(4) 'Confidentiality' - the agent must keep private information provided by the principal and information which would give a

customer an advantage over the principal strictly confidential, unless the agent has the principal's permission to disclose the information. This duty lives on after the agency relationship is terminated.

(5) 'Reasonable skill, care and diligence' - the agent must perform all duties with the care and diligence which may be reasonably expected of someone undertaking such duties.

(6) 'Full accounting' - the agent must provide a full accounting of any money or 10

goods coming into the agent's possession which belong to the principal or other parties.

H. "First Substantive Meeting" shall be:

(1) In a real estate transaction in which the Broker is the agent for the seller, first substantive meeting shall be before or just immediately prior to the first of any of the following:

(a) Showing the property to a prospective buyer.

(b) Eliciting confidential information from a buyer concerning the buyers' real estate needs, motivation, or financial qualifications.

(c) The execution of any agreements governed by Section 73-35-3 of the Mississippi Code of 1972 Annotated.

(2) For the seller's agent, the definition shall not include:

(a) A bona fide "open house" or model home showing which encompasses (1) (a) above only; however, whenever an event described in (1) (b) or (1) (c) occurs, disclosure must be made.

(b) Preliminary conversations or "small talk" concerning price range, location and property styles.

(c) Responding to general factual questions from a prospective buyer concerning properties that have been advertised for sale or lease.

(3) In a real estate transaction in which the Broker is the agent for the buyer, first substantive meeting shall be at the initial contact with a seller or a seller's agent or before or just immediately prior to the first of any of the following:

(a) Showing the property of a seller to a represented buyer.

(b) Eliciting any confidential information from a seller concerning their real estate needs, motivation, or financial qualifications.

(c) The execution of any agreements governed by Section 73-35-3 of the MS Code.

(4) For the buyer's agent, the definition shall not include:

(a) A bona fide "open House" or model home showing which encompasses (3) (a) above only; however, whenever an event described in (3) (b) or (3) (c) occurs, disclosure must be made.

(b) Preliminary conversations or "small talk" concerning price range, location and property styles.

(c) Responding to general factual questions from a prospective buyer concerning properties that have been advertised for sale or lease.

I. "Single Agency" shall mean a broker who has chosen to represent only one party to a real estate transaction. It may be either the buyer, seller, lessor or lessee or any party in a transaction governed by Section 73-35-3.

Source: § Source: Miss. Code Ann. §§ 73-35-3

Rule 4.3 Disclosure Requirements

A. In a single agency, a broker is required to disclose, in writing, to the party for whom the broker is an agent in a real estate transaction that the broker is the agent of the party. The written disclosure must be made before the time an agreement for representation is entered into between the broker and the party. This shall be on an MREC Agency Disclosure Form.

B. In a single agency, a real estate broker is required to disclose, in writing, to the party for whom the broker is not an agent, that the broker is an agent of another party in the transaction. The written disclosure shall be made at the time of the first substantive meeting with the party for whom the broker is not an agent. This shall be on an MREC Agency Disclosure Form.

C. Brokers operating in the capacity of disclosed dual agents must obtain the informed written consent of all parties prior to or at the time of formalization of the dual agency. Informed written consent to disclosed dual agency shall be deemed to have been timely obtained if all of the following occur:

(1) The seller, at the time an agreement for representation is entered into between the broker and seller, gives written consent to dual agency by signing the Consent To Dual Agency portion of MREC Form A.

(2) The buyer, at the time an agreement for representation is entered into between the broker and buyer, gives written consent to dual agency by signing the Consent To Dual Agency portion of MREC Form A.

(3) The Broker must confirm that the buyer(s) understands and consents to the consensual dual agency relationship prior to the signing of an offer to purchase. The buyer shall give his/her consent by signing the MREC Dual Agency Confirmation Form which shall be attached to the offer to purchase. The Broker must

confirm that the seller(s) also understands and consents to the consensual dual agency relationship prior to presenting the offer to purchase. The seller shall give his/her consent by signing the MREC Dual Agency Confirmation Form attached to the buyer's offer. The form shall remain attached to the offer to purchase regardless of the outcome of the offer to purchase.

D. In the event the agency relationship changes between the parties to a real estate transaction, new disclosure forms will be acknowledged by all parties involved.

E. In the event one or more parties are not available to sign one or more of the Disclosure Forms, the disclosure will be accomplished orally. The applicable form will be so noted by the Broker and said forms will be forwarded for signature(s) as soon as possible. Written electronic transmission will fulfill this requirement.

F. In the event any party receiving a disclosure form requests not to sign that form acknowledging receipt, the Broker shall annotate the form with the following statement:

"A COPY OF THIS FORM WAS DELIVERED TO _____ DATE_____. RECIPIENT DECLINED TO ACKNOWLEDGE RECEIPT OF THIS FORM."

G. The terms of the agency relationship shall be ratified on all contracts pertaining to real estate transactions.

H. The Commission mandated disclosure form may be duplicated in content and size but not altered.

I. Completed Agency Disclosure Forms shall be maintained in accordance with Rules and Regulations IV. B (6).

Source: Source: Miss. Code Ann. §§ 73-35-3

Rule 4.4 Disclosure Exception

A licensee shall not be required to comply with the provisions of Section 3, when engaged in transactions with any corporation, non-profit corporation, professional corporation, professional association, limited liability company, partnership, real estate investment trust, business trust, charitable trust, family trust, or any governmental entity in transactions involving real estate.

Operating under this exception in no way circumvents the common law of agency.

Source: Miss. Code Ann. §§ 73-35-35

Part 1601 Chapter 5: Complaint Procedure

Rule 5.1 Notifications of Complaints to the Commission

A. All complaints submitted to the Commission shall be properly certified on forms furnished by the Commission.

B. Every licensee shall, within ten days, notify the Real Estate Commission of any adverse court decisions in which the licensee appeared as a defendant.

C. It shall be mandatory for a responsible broker to notify the Commission if the responsible broker has reason to believe that a licensee for whom the broker is responsible has violated the Real Estate License Law or Rules and Regulations of the Commission.

D. If a broker finds that a licensee licensed under that broker has been operating independently or through some other broker, the broker shall notify the Commission immediately and forward said individual's license to the Commission.

E. A Real Estate Commissioner shall avoid private interviews, arguments, briefs or communication that may influence said Commissioner's decision on any pending complaints or hearings.

F. The expiration, suspension or revocation of a responsible broker's license shall automatically suspend the license of every real estate licensee currently under the supervision of that broker. In such cases, a licensee may transfer to another responsible broker.

Source: Miss. Code Ann. §§ 73-35-35

Part 1601 Chapter 6: Continuing Education

Rule 6.1 Approved Courses

A. Any course that meets the educational requirements as set forth in Section 73-35-7 of the Mississippi Real Estate Broker's License Act of 1954, as Amended.

B. Any course sponsored or provided by the Mississippi Real Estate Commission.

C. Any course which has been individually approved by the Commission pursuant to the provisions of this rule and which must be approved prior to presentation of the course, except that, in the Commission's discretion, courses which have not received such prior approval but which meet the proper criteria may be approved for credit for licensees who have completed such course.

D. Any course which has been approved for real estate continuing education by any state or country which is a member of the Association of Real Estate License Law Officials (ARELLO) and which course satisfies the requirements set forth in Rule VI (B) (3) with the exception of instruction in license law which pertains solely to a state other than Mississippi.

Source: Miss. Code Ann. §§ 73-35-35 14

Rule 6.2 Procedures and Criteria for Approval of Courses

A. Definitions:

(1) "Provider" - any individual person, partnership, association, legally established corporation or LLC, educational organization, or other entity that sponsors, offers, organizes, provides or promotes real estate continuing education courses.

(2) "Instructor" - a person who delivers educational material information directly to students.

B. A provider desiring approval of continuing education course referred to in Section 73-35- 18, Mississippi Code of 1972, Annotated, shall make application to the Commission on forms provided by the Commission. The provider, course, and instructor must receive concurrent approval.

C. All requests for course accreditation shall be submitted on forms provided by MREC and will require copies of all student materials as well as documentation that includes the following:

(1) Course descriptions of each subject in the course.

(2) Measurable learning objectives for each subject.

(3) Specific process for evaluation and improvement of content.

(4) Specific processes for selecting and evaluating instructors.

(5) Specific processes for record-keeping and the administration of examinations.

D. For courses offered through distance learning:

(1) Courses in Mississippi license law, contract law, and agency shall include course content and application specific to Mississippi practice and custom.

(2) Out-of-state providers must provide copies or screen prints of all Mississippi specific content for MREC review and approval.

(3) On-line or CD-ROM courses relating to Mississippi license law and agency must include instruction in the use of the Mississippi mandatory forms as well as provide a mechanism for the student to view and download the forms.

E. Standards for approval of course:

(1) A proposed continuing education course shall be a real estate oriented educational session or course intended to improve skills of licensees and to keep licensees abreast of changing real estate practices and laws.

(2) Courses shall be taught only by approved, qualified instructors.

(3) Courses shall be offered in minimum two-hour segments.

(4) Courses, instructors and providers shall be approved for one (1) year periods and shall be required to renew if the course is to be continued.

(5) Licensees shall physically attend in order to receive a certificate.

Source: Miss. Code Ann. §§ 73-35-35

Rule 6.3 Qualifications of Instructors

The education and experience of the instructor must be appropriate to teach the subject matter.

Source: Miss. Code Ann. §§ 73-35-35

Rule 6.4 Administrative Requirements - Applies to VI A. 2. & 3.

A. Providers of continuing education courses shall furnish the Commission with a class roster within thirty (30) days after completion of each course listing each Mississippi licensee in attendance in alphabetical order.

B. Providers will utilize a three-part certificate for the purpose of certifying individual attendance. One designated part shall be returned completed to the commission, one designated part shall be given to each attendee at the conclusion of the course, and the remaining par shall be retained by the provider furnishing such information as may be called for on the certificate.

C. Attendance and other records of each provider must be kept on file for a period of three years and are subject to inspection by the Commission at any time during normal business hours.

Source: Miss. Code Ann. §§ 73-35-35

Rule 6.5 Advertising and solicitation

A. An approved real estate provider must include, in all forms of advertising, the school's name and the physical location of its principal place of business.

B. An approved real estate provider may not advertise through oral statements or written text in such a manner that the statement is included or contained in any advertisement by a real estate broker and no advertisement of a licensed school may refer to the brokerage operation or include the telephone number of any individual broker.

C. An approved real estate provider may not:

(1) Indicate any name other than the name approved by the Mississippi Real Estate Commission (MREC).

(2) Indicate that it has been endorsed, recommended, or certified

by the MREC except that the provider may advertise that it is approved by the MREC to provide instruction in real estate courses.

(3) Indicate that successful completion of its curriculum will result in passing a real estate licensing exam, may not make any guarantee of employment to a student or prospective student, and may not promote the business or any real estate licensee, real estate franchise, or network.

Source: Miss. Code Ann. §§ 73-35-35

Rule 6.6 Relationship with providers

A. No real estate education presentation may be conducted in a facility that is also utilized for conducting the business of real estate brokerage unless all participants are licensees of the brokerage firm conducting the courses.

B. No real estate education provider will allow in-person or electronic solicitation of students for employment. A provider may not post, distribute, or display written material concerning employment nor use any approved course for the purpose of discussing, inducting, or promoting affiliation with any broker or brokerage firm during the prescribed class hours nor during the breaks between such class hours.

C. Providers may advertise that a course meets a portion of the continuing education requirements; however, no advertisement shall be used which states or implies that the Mississippi Real Estate Commission has approved or passed on the merits of a course.

Source: Miss. Code Ann. §§ 73-35-35

Rule 6.7 Suspension or Revocation of Approval

Failure to comply with any provision of this rule shall constitute grounds for suspension or revocation of the approval of a course, a provider or an instructor, or other such action as deemed appropriate by the Commission.

Source: Miss. Code Ann. §§ 73-35-35

Part 1601 Chapter 7: INSPECTION OF OFFERINGS FROM OUT OF STATE 17

Rule 7.1 Out-of-state Developers

Out-of-state land developers who desire to advertise out-of-state property in Mississippi (except in national publications) shall first contact the Mississippi Real Estate Commission to have the property approved for advertising. The Mississippi Real Estate Commission may in its discretion conduct an on-site inspection of the property at the cost of the developer. The developer shall, upon request from the Mississippi Real Estate Commission, provide such documentation which will establish the truth and accuracy of the proposed advertisements. A Mississippi broker who becomes the agent or representative of the out-of-state developer, shall be responsible for the truth and accuracy of representation, offerings and advertising of such properties in the State of Mississippi.

Source: Miss. Code Ann. §§ 73-35-35

Part 1601 Chapter 8: Time Shares

Rule 8.1 Licensing

Any seller, other than the developer and its regular employees, of a timeshare plan within the State of Mississippi must be a licensed Real Estate Broker or Real Estate Salesperson pursuant to and subject to Mississippi Law and the Rules and Regulations of the Mississippi Real Estate Commission.

Source: Miss. Code Ann. §§ 73-35-35

Rule 8.2 Definitions

A. "Accommodations" means any structure, service improvement, facility, apartment, condominium or cooperative unit, cabin, lodge, hotel or motel room, or any other private or commercial structure, which is situated on real property and designed for occupancy by one or more individuals.

B. "Advertising" or "Advertisement" means any written, oral, or electronic communication which contains a promotion, inducement, or offer to sell a timeshare plan, including, but not limited to, brochures, pamphlets, radio and television scripts, electronic media, telephone and direct mail solicitations, and other means of promotion.

C. "Assessment" means the share of funds required for the payment of common expenses that are assessed from time to time against each timeshare interest owner by the managing entity.

D. "Association" means the organized body consisting of the owners of timeshare interests in a timeshare plan.

E. "Common Expenses" means taxes, casualty and liability insurance, and those expenses properly incurred for the maintenance, operation, and repair of all accommodations constituting the timeshare plan and any other expenses designated as common expenses by the timeshare instrument.

F. "Developer" means and includes any person who creates a timeshare plan or is in the business of selling timeshare interests, or employs agents to do the same, or any person who succeeds to the interest of a developer by sale, lease, assignment, mortgage, or other transfer, but the term includes only those persons who offer timeshare interests for disposition in the ordinary course of business and does not include those sellers who sell timeshare interests on the developer's behalf.

G. "Managing entity" means the natural person or other entity that undertakes the duties, responsibilities, and obligations of the management of a timeshare plan.

H. "Exchange program" means any method, arrangement, or procedure for the voluntary exchange of timeshare interests or other property interests. The term does not include the assignment of the right to use and occupy accommodations to owners of timeshare interests within a timeshare plan. Any method, arrangement, or procedure that otherwise meets this definition in which the purchaser's total contractual financial obligation exceeds three thousand dollars ($3,000) per any individual, recurring timeshare period, shall be regulated as a timeshare plan in accordance with these rules. For purposes of determining the purchaser's total contractual financial obligation, amounts to be paid as a result of renewals and options to renew shall be included except for the following:

(1) the amounts to be paid as a result of any optional renewal that a purchaser, in his or her sole discretion may elect to exercise or

(2) the amounts to be paid as a result of any automatic renewal in which the purchaser has a right to terminate during the renewal period at any time and receive a pro rata refund for the remaining unexpired renewal term or

(3) amounts to be paid as a result of an automatic renewal wherein the purchaser receives a written notice no less than 30 nor more than 90 days prior to the date of renewal informing the purchaser of the right to terminate prior to the date of renewal.

Notwithstanding these exceptions, if the contractual financial obligation exceeds three thousand dollars ($3,000) for any three-year period of any renewal term, amounts to be paid as a result of that renewal shall be included in determining the purchaser's total contractual financial obligation.

I. "Offer to sell", "offer for sale," "offered for sale," or "offer" means solicitation of purchasers, the taking of reservations, or any other method whereby a purchaser is offered the opportunity to participate in a timeshare plan.

J. "Purchaser" means any person, other than a developer, who by means of a voluntary transfer for consideration acquires a legal or equitable interest in a timeshare plan other than as security for an obligation.

K. "Reservation system" means the method or arrangement which purchasers are required to utilize in order to reserve the use and occupancy of accommodations in a timeshare plan.

L. "Seller" means any developer or any other person, or agent or employee thereof: who offers timeshare periods for sale to the public in the ordinary course of business, except a person who has acquired a timeshare period for the person's own use and occupancy and who later offers it for resale.

M. "Timeshare instrument" means one or more documents, by whatever name denominated, creating or governing the operation of a timeshare plan and includes the declaration or other legal instrument dedicating the accommodations to the timeshare plan.

N. "Timeshare interest" means and includes either of the following:

(1) A "timeshare estate," which is the right to occupy a timeshare property, coupled with a freehold estate or an estate for years with

a future interest in a timeshare property or a specified portion thereof.

(2) A "timeshare plan" which is the right to occupy a timeshare property, which right is neither coupled with a freehold interest, nor coupled with an estate for years with a future interest, in a timeshare property.

O. "Timeshare plan" means any arrangement, plan, scheme, or similar device, other than an exchange program, whether by membership agreement, sale, lease, deed, license, right to use agreement, or by any other means, whereby a purchaser, in exchange for consideration, receives ownership rights in or the right to use accommodations for a period of time less than a full year during any given year, on a recurring basis for more than one year, but not necessarily for consecutive years. A timeshare plan may be either of the following:

(1) A "single-site timeshare plan" which is the right to use accommodations at a single timeshare property; or

(2) A "multi-site timeshare plan" that includes either of the following:

(a) A "specific timeshare interest" which is the right to use accommodations at a specific timeshare property, together with use rights in accommodations at one or more other component sites created by or acquired through the timeshare plan's reservation system; or

(b) A "non-specific timeshare interest" which is the right to use accommodations at more than one component site created by or acquired through the timeshare plan's reservation system, but including no right to 20 use any specific accommodation.

P. "Timeshare property" means one or more accommodations subject to the same timeshare instrument, together with any other property or rights to property appurtenant to those accommodations.

Q. "Mississippi Real Estate Commission," or "Commission" means the agency of the State of Mississippi created by §73-35-1, *et seq.* To regulate the licensing of real estate brokers and salespersons and by §73-35-35 directed to regulate the sale of timeshare and condominium properties.

Source: Miss. Code Ann. §§ 73-35-35

Rule 8.3 Registration

A. Developer registration; offer or disposal of interest. - A developer, or any of its agents, shall not sell, offer or dispose of a timeshare interest in the state unless all necessary registration requirements are completed and approved by the Mississippi Real Estate Commission, or the sale, offer, or disposition is otherwise permitted by or exempt from these rules. A developer, or any of its agents, shall not sell, offer or dispose of a timeshare interest in the state while an order revoking or suspending a registration is in effect.

B. Exemptions from developer registration

(1) A person is exempt from the registration requirements under the following circumstances.

(a) An owner of a timeshare interest who has acquired the timeshare interest from another for the owner's own use and occupancy and who later offers it for resale; or

(b) A managing entity or an association that is offering to sell one or more timeshare interests acquired through foreclosure, deed in lieu of foreclosure or gratuitous transfer, if such acts are performed in the regular course of or as incident to the management of the association for its own account in the timeshare plan; or

(c) The person offers a timeshare plan located outside of Mississippi in a national publication or by electronic media, which is not directed to or targeted to any individual located in Mississippi and contains appropriate disclaimers; or

(d) The person is conveyed, assigned, or transferred more than seven timeshare interests from a developer in a single voluntary or involuntary transaction arid subsequently conveys, assigns, or transfers all of the timeshare interests received from the developer to a single purchaser in a single transaction.

(e) (i) The developer is offering a timeshare interest to a purchaser who has previously acquired a timeshare interest from the same developer if the developer has a timeshare plan registered with the Commission, which was originally approved by the Commission within the preceding seven (7) years and, further, provides the purchaser:

(A) a cancellation period of at least seven (7) calendar days;

(B) all the timeshare disclosure documents that are required to be provided to purchasers as if the sale occurred in the state or jurisdiction where the timeshare property is located; and

(ii) By making such an offering or disposition, the person is deemed to consent to the jurisdiction of the Commission in the event of a dispute with the purchaser in connection with the offering or disposition.

(f) An offering of any plan in which the purchaser's total financial obligation is $3,000 or less during the term of the plan; for purposes of determining the purchaser's total financial obligation, all amounts to be paid during any renewal or periods of optional renewal shall be included.

(g) Hotels including any hotel, inn, motel, tourist court, apartment house, rooming house, or other place where sleeping accommodations are furnished or offered for pay if four (4) or more rooms are available therein for transient guests as defined in Miss. Code Ann. §41-49-3.

(h) Campground, which is located on real property, made available to persons for camping, whether by tent, trailer, camper, cabin, recreational vehicle or similar device and shall include the outdoor recreational facilities located on the real property;

(i) Hunting camp which means land or facilities located on real property which is established for the principal purpose of hunting or fishing activities which are subject to licensing by the State of Mississippi pursuant to Miss. Code Ann. §49-7-1, *et seq.*

(j) Owner referrals as described in Section N of these rules.

C. Developer Registration Requirements

(1) Any person who, to any individual in Mississippi, sells, offers to sell, or attempts to solicit prospective purchasers to purchase a timeshare interest, or any person who creates a timeshare plan with an accommodation in Mississippi must register the timeshare plan with the Commission unless the timeshare plan is otherwise exempt from this Chapter.

(2) The developer shall have the duty to supervise and control all aspects of the offering of a timeshare plan including, but not limited to the promotion, advertising, contracting and closing.

(3) The developer must provide proof as part of the registration that he will comply with escrow, bonding, or other financial

assurance requirements for purchaser funds, including escrow during the rescission period, escrow funds until substantial completion, or bonding, letter of credit or other financial assurances acceptable to the Commission.

(4) All timeshare plans shall maintain a one-to-one purchaser to accommodation ratio, which is the ratio of the number of purchasers eligible to use the accommodations of a timeshare plan on a given day to the number of accommodations available for use within the plan on that day, such that the total number of purchasers eligible to use the accommodations of the timeshare plan during a given calendar year never exceeds the total number of accommodations available for use in the timeshare plan during that year. For purposes of calculation under this subsection, each purchaser must be counted at least once, and no individual timeshare unit may be counted more than 365 times per calendar year (or more than 366 times per leap year). A purchaser who is delinquent in the payment of timeshare plan assessments shall continue to be considered eligible to use the accommodations of the timeshare plan.

D. Comprehensive registration

(1) In registering a timeshare plan, the developer shall provide all of the following information:

(a) The developer's legal name, any assumed names used by the developer, principal office, street address, mailing address, primary contact person, telephone, electronic mail and facsimile numbers;

(b) The name of the developer's authorized or registered agent in Mississippi upon whom claims may be served or service of process be had, the agent's street address in Mississippi and telephone number;

(c) The name, street address, mailing address, primary contact person and telephone, electronic mail and facsimile numbers of any timeshare plans being registered;

(d) The name, street address, mailing address and telephone, electronic mail and facsimile numbers of any managing entity of the timeshare plan if other than the developer;

(e) Current status of title by a title insurance company qualified and registered to do business in Mississippi, or in the jurisdiction where the timeshare plan is located;

(f) A copy of the proposed or existing covenants, conditions and restrictions applicable to the timeshare plan;

(g) Exemplars of all contracts, deeds, fact sheets and other instruments to be used in marketing, financing and conveying the timeshare interests;

(h) A copy of the management agreement for the timeshare plan;

(i) A detailed description of the furnishing(s) and other personal property to be included in the timeshare plans;

(j) Agreement of the developer to subsidize maintenance and operation of the timeshare plan, if any;

(k) Description of other services and amenities advertised with the timesharing plan;

(l) Evidence of financial assurances, if any;

(m) Evidence of compliance with escrow or other financial assurance requirements for protection of purchaser funds pursuant to these rules.

(n) Where the timeshare plan uses a reservation system, the developer shall provide evidence that provisions are in place to assure that, in the event of termination of the operator of the reservation system, an adequate period of continued operation exists to assure a transition to a substitute operator or mechanism for the operation of the reservation system. In addition, there shall be a requirements to transfer all relevant data contained in the reservation system to the successor operator of the system.

(o) A description of the inventory control system that will ensure compliance with subsection 3.c. of this section.

(p) A public offering statement which complies with the requirements set forth below; and

(q) Any other information regarding the developer, timeshare plan, or managing entities, as reasonably required by the Commission for the protection of the purchasers.

E. Abbreviated Registration

(1) The Commission may accept an abbreviated application from a developer of a timeshare plan in which all accommodations are located outside of the state. A developer of a timeshare plan with any accommodation located in Mississippi may not file an abbreviated filing, with the exception of a succeeding developer after a merger or acquisition when the developer's timeshare plan was registered in the state immediately preceding the merger or acquisition.

(2) As a part of any application for an abbreviated registration, the developer must provide a certificate of registration or other evidence of registration from the appropriate regulatory agency in the jurisdiction in which the accommodations offered in Mississippi are located, or other evidence of compliance by the timeshare plan with the laws of the jurisdiction where the

accommodations are located. Such other jurisdiction must have disclosure requirements that are substantially equivalent or greater than the information required to be disclosed to purchasers by these rules. A developer filing an abbreviated registration application must also provide the following:

(a) The developer's name, any assumed names used by the developer, the developer's principal office location, mailing address, primary contact person and telephone, electronic mail and facsimile numbers;

(b) The name, location, mailing address, primary contact person and the telephone, electronic mail and facsimile numbers of the timeshare plan, if different from the developer;

(c) The name of the authorized agent or registered agent in Mississippi upon whom claims can be served or service of process can be had, and the address in Mississippi of the authorized agent or registered agent;

(d) The names of any sales entity if other than the developer and the managing' entity and their principal office locations, mailing address and telephone, electronic mail and facsimile numbers;

(e) A statement as to whether the timeshare plan is a single-site timeshare plan or a multi-site timeshare plan and, if a multi-site timeshare plan, whether it consists of specific timeshare interests or non-specific timeshare interests;

(f) Disclosure of each jurisdiction in which the developer has applied for registration of the timeshare plan and whether the timeshare plan, its developer or any of its sales agents or managing entities utilized were denied registration or were the subject of any disciplinary proceedings;

(g) Copies of any disclosure documents required to be given to purchasers or required to be filed with the jurisdiction in which the timeshare plan is approved or accepted as may be requested by the Commission;

(h) The appropriate fees, if any, and

(i) Other information reasonably required by the Commission or established by rule.

F. Preliminary Permits

(1) The state may grant a preliminary permit allowing the developer to begin offering and selling timeshare interests while the registration is in process. To obtain a preliminary permit, the developer must do all of the following:

(a) Submit a formal written request to the Mississippi Real Estate Commission for a preliminary permit;

(b) Submit a substantially complete application for registration to the Commission, including any appropriate fees and exhibits;

(c) Provide evidence acceptable to the state agency that all funds received by the developer will be placed into an independent escrow account in accordance with the escrow requirements until a final registration has been granted;

(d) Give to each purchaser a copy of the proposed public offering statement that the developer has submitted to the Commission with the initial application; and

(e) Give to each purchaser the opportunity to cancel the purchase contract during the applicable rescission period. The purchaser shall have an additional opportunity to cancel upon the issuance of an approved registration if the Commission determines that there is a material and adverse difference in the disclosures contained in the final public offering statement and those given to the purchaser in the proposed public offering statement.

Source: Miss. Code Ann. §§ 73-35-35

Rule 8.4 Public Offering Statement

A. Public Offering Statement Requirements

(1) A developer must prepare a public offering statement that shall fully and accurately disclose the facts concerning the timeshare developer and timeshare plan as required by these rules. The developer shall provide the public offering statement to each purchaser of a timeshare interest in any timeshare plan prior to execution of the purchase contract. The public offering statement shall be dated and shall require the purchaser to certify in writing the receipt thereof. Upon approval by the Commission, the developer may also deliver the public offering statement on CD ROM or other electronic media.

(2) With regard to timeshare interests offered in a single-site timeshare plan or in the specific interest of a multi-site timeshare plan, the public offering statement should fully and accurately disclose the following:

(a) The name of the developer and the principal address of the developer;

(b) Information regarding the developer's business and property management experience;

(c) A description of the type of timeshare interests being offered;

(d) The number of accommodations and timeshare interests, expressed in periods of seven-days use availability or other time increments applicable to the multi-site timeshare plan for each component site committed to the multi-site timeshare plan and available for use by purchasers, purchasers and a representation about the percentage of useable time authorized for sale, and if that percentage is 100 percent, then a statement describing how adequate periods of time for maintenance and repair will be provided. A general description of the existing and proposed accommodations and amenities of the timeshare plan, including their type and number personal property furnishing the accommodation, any use restrictions, and any required fees for use;

(e) A description of any accommodations and amenities that are committed to be built, including, without limitation:

(i) the developer's schedule of commencement and completion of all accommodations and amenities;

(ii) the estimated number of accommodations per site that may become subject to the timeshare plan;

(iii) a brief description of the duration, phases, and operation of the timeshare plan; and

(iv) the extent to which financial arrangements have been provided for completion of all promised improvements.

(f) If the timeshare plan requires the use of a reservation system, include a description of the reservation system which shall include the following:

(i) The entity responsible for operating the reservation system, its relationship to the developer, and the duration of any agreement for operation of the reservation system.

(ii) A summary of the rules and regulations governing access to and use of the reservation system.

(iii) The existence of and an explanation regarding any priority reservation features that affect a purchaser's ability to make reservations for the use of a given accommodation on a first-come, first-serve basis.

(iv) An explanation of any demand-balancing standard utilized to assure equitable use of the accommodations among participants.

(g) The current annual budget, if available, or the projected annual budget for the timeshare plan. The budget must include, without limitations:

(i) a statement of the amount included in the budget as a reserve for repairs and replacement;

(ii) the projected common expense liability, if any, by category of expenditures for the timeshare plan; and

(iii) a statement of any services or expenses not reflected in the budget that the developer provides or pays.

(h) Information regarding all fees that the purchaser is required to pay in conjunction with the purchase and ownership including, but not limited to, closing cost and annual assessments;

(i) A description of any liens, defects or encumbrances on or affecting the title to the timeshare interests;

(j) A description of any financing offered by or available through the developer;

(k) A statement that within seven (7) calendar days after receipt of the public offering statement or after execution of the purchase contract, whichever is later, a purchaser may cancel any purchase contract for a timeshare interest from a developer together with a statement providing the name and street address to which the purchaser shall mail any notice of cancellation. If by agreement of the parties by and through the purchase contract, the purchase contract allows for cancellation of the purchase contract for a period of time exceeding seven (7) calendar days, then the public offering statement shall include a statement that the cancellation of the purchase contract is allowing for that period of time exceeding seven (7) calendar days;

(l) A description of any bankruptcies, pending civil or criminal suits, adjudications, or disciplinary actions of which the developer has knowledge, which would have a material effect on the developer's ability to perform its obligations.

(m) Any restrictions on alienation of any number or portion of any timeshare interests;

(n) A statement describing liability and casualty insurance for the timeshare property;

(o) Any current or expected fees or charges to be paid by timeshare purchasers for the use of any amenities related to the timeshare plan;

(p) A statement disclosing any right of first refusal or other restraint on the transfer of all or any portion of a timeshare interest.

(q) A statement of disclosing that any deposit made in connection which the purchase of a timeshare interest shall be held by an escrow agent until expiration of any right to cancel the contract and that any deposit shall be returned to the purchaser if he or she elects to exercise his or her right of cancellation. Alternatively, if the Commission has accepted from the developer a surety bond, irrevocable letter of credit, or other financial assurance in lieu of placing deposits in an escrow account, account:

(i) a statement disclosing that the developer has provided a surety bond, irrevocable letter of credit, or other financial assurance in an amount equal to or in excess of the funds that would otherwise be placed in an escrow account and,

(ii) a description of the type of financial assurance that has been arranged,

(iii) a statement that if the purchaser elects to exercise his or her right of cancellation as provided in the contract, the developer shall return the deposit, and

(iv) a description of the person or entity to whom the purchaser shall apply for payment.

(r) If the timeshare plan provides purchasers with the opportunity to participate in an exchange program, a description of the name and address of the exchange company and the method by which a purchaser accesses the exchange program;

(s) Such other information reasonable required by the state agency and established by administrative rule necessary for the protection of purchasers of timeshare interests in timeshare plans; and

(t) Any other information that the developer, with the approval of the Commission, desires to include in the public offering statement.

(3) Public offering statements for specific timeshare interest and multi-site timeshare plans shall include the following disclosures in addition to those required in (b) above:

(a) A description of each component site, including the name and address of each Component site.

(b) The number of accommodations and timeshare interest, expressed in periods of seven-day use availability or other time increments applicable to each component site of the timeshare plan, committed to the multi-site timeshare plan and available for use by purchasers, and a representation about the percentage of useable time authorized for sale, and if that percentage is 100 percent, then a statement describing how adequate periods of time for maintenance and repair will be provided.

(c) Each type of accommodation in terms of the number of bedrooms, bathrooms, and sleeping capacity, and a statement of whether or not the accommodation contains a full kitchen. For purposes of this description, a "full kitchen" means a kitchen having a minimum of a dishwasher, range, sink, oven, and refrigerator.

(d) A description of amenities available for use by the purchaser at each component site.

(e) A description of the reservation system, which shall include the following:

(i) The entity responsible for operating the reservation systems, its relationship to the developer, and the duration of any agreement for operation of the reservation system.

(ii) A summary of the rules and regulations governing access to and use of the reservation system.

(iii) The existence of and an explanation regarding any priority reservations for the use of a given accommodation on a first-come, first-served basis.

(iv) An explanation of any demand-balancing standard utilized to assure equitable use of the accommodations among participants.

(v) A description of any method utilized to permit additions, substitutions, or deletions of accommodations.

(vi) A description of any criteria utilized in the use and operation of the reservation system (such as historical occupancy levels by season, location, demand, etc.)

(f) The name and principal address of the managing entity of the multi-site timeshare plan and description of the procedures, if any, for altering the powers and responsibilities of the managing entity and for removing or replacing it.

(g) A description of any right to make any addition, substitutions, or deletion of accommodations, amenities, or component sites, and a description of the basis upon which accommodations, amenities, or component sites may be added to, substituted in, or deleted from the multi-site timeshare plan.

(h) A description of the purchaser's liability for any fees associated with the multi-site timeshare plan.

(i) The location of each component site of the multi-site timeshare plan, the historical occupancy of each component site for the prior 12-month period, if the component site was part of the multi-site timeshare plan during the 12-month time period, as well as any periodic adjustment or amendment to the reservation system that may be needed in order to respond to actual purchaser use patterns and changes in purchaser use demand for the accommodations existing at that time within the multi-site timeshare plan.

(j) Any other information that the developer, with the approval of the Commission, desires to include in the timeshare disclosure statement.

(4) Public offering statements for nonspecific timeshare multi-site timeshare plans shall include the following:

(a) The name and address of the developer.

(b) A description of the type of interest and usage rights the purchaser will receive.

(c) A description of the duration and operation of the timeshare plan.

(d) A description of the type of insurance coverage provided for each component site.

(e) An explanation of who holds title to the accommodations of each component site.

(f) A description of each component site, including the name and address of each component site.

(g) The number of accommodations and timeshare interest, expressed in periods of seven-day use availability or other time increments applicable to the multi-site timeshare plan for each component site committed to the multi-site timeshare plan and available for use by purchasers. purchasers and a representation about the percentage of useable time authorized for sale, and if that percentage is 100 percent, then a statement describing how adequate periods of time for maintenance and repair will be provided.

(h) Each type of accommodation in terms of the number of bedrooms, bathrooms, and sleeping capacity, and a statement of whether or not the accommodation contains a full kitchen. For purposes of this description, a "full kitchen" means a kitchen having a minimum of a dishwasher, range, sink, oven, and refrigerator.

(i) A description of amenities available for use by the purchaser at each component site.

(j) A description of any incomplete amenities at any of the component sites along with a statement as to any assurance for completion and the estimated date the amenities will be available.

(k) The location of each component site of the multi-site timeshare plan, the historical occupancy of each component site for the prior 12-month period, if the component site was part of the multi-site timeshare plan during such 12-month time period, as well as any periodic adjustment or amendments to the reservation system that may be needed in order to respond to actual purchaser use patterns and changes in purchaser use demand for the accommodations existing at that time within the multi-site timeshare plan.

(l) A description of any rights to make any additions, substitutions, or deletions of accommodations, amenities, or component sites, and a description of the basis upon which accommodations, amenities, or component sites may be added to, substituted in, or deleted form the multi-site timeshare plan.

(m) A description of the reservation system that shall include all of the following:

(i) The entity responsible for operating the reservation system, its relationship to the developer, and the duration of any agreement for operation of the reservation system.

(ii) A summary of the rules and regulations governing access to and use of the reservation system.

(iii) The existence of and an explanation regarding any priority reservation features that affect a purchaser's ability to make reservations for the use of a given accommodation on a first-come, first-served basis.

(n) The name and principal address of the managing entity for the multi-site timeshare plan and a description of the procedures, if any, for altering the powers and responsibilities of the managing entity and for removing or replacing it, and a description of the relationship between a multi-site timeshare plan managing entity and the managing entity of the component sites of a multi-site timeshare plan, if different from the multi-site timeshare plan managing entity.

(o) The current annual budget as provided in Section L. of these rules, along with the projected assessments and a description of the method of calculation and apportioning the assessments among purchasers, all of which shall be attached as an exhibit to the public offering statement.

(p) Any current fees or charges to be paid by timeshare purchasers for the use of any amenities related to the timeshare plan and statement that the fees or charges are subject to change.

(q) Any initial or special fee due from the purchaser at closing, together with a description of the purpose and method of calculating the fee.

(r) A description of any financing offered by or available through the developer.

(s) A description of any bankruptcies, pending civil or criminal suits, adjudications, or disciplinary actions of which the developer has knowledge, which would have a material effect on the developer's ability to perform its obligations.

(t) A statement disclosing any right of first refusal or other restraint on the transfer of all or any portion of a timeshare interest.

(u) A statement disclosing that any deposit made in connection with the purchase of a timeshare interest shall be held by an escrow agent until expiration of any right to cancel the contract and that any deposit shall be returned to the purchaser if he or she elects to exercise his or her right of cancellation. Alternatively, if the Commission has accepted from the developer a surety bond, irrevocable letter of credit, or other financial assurance in lieu of placing deposits in an escrow account, account:

(i) a statement disclosing that the developer has provided a surety bond, irrevocable letter of credit, or other financial assurance in an amount equal to or in excess of the funds that would otherwise be placed in an escrow account and,

(ii) a description of the type of financial assurance that has been arranged,

(iii) a statement that if the purchaser elects to exercise his or her right of cancellation as provided in the contract, the developer shall return the deposit, and

(iv) a description of the person or entity to whom the purchaser should apply for payment.

(v) If the timeshare plan provides purchasers with the opportunity to participate in an exchange program, a description of the name and address of the exchange company and the method by which a purchaser accesses the exchange program.

(w) Any other information that the developer, with the approval of the Commission, desires to include in the timeshare disclosure statement.

Source: Miss. Code Ann. §§ 73-35-35

Rule 8.5 Amendment to Registration Information and Public Offering Statement:

The developer shall amend or supplement its Public Offering Statement and registration information to reflect any material change in any information contained therein. All such amendments, supplements and changes shall be filed with and approved by the Commission. Each approved amendment to the Public Offering Statement, other than an amendment made only for the purpose of the addition of a phase or phases to the timeshare plan in the manner described in the timeshare instrument or any amendment that does not materially alter or modify the offering in a manner that is adverse to a purchaser, shall be delivered to a purchaser no later than 10 days prior to closing.

Source: Miss. Code Ann. §§ 73-35-35

Rule 8.6 Registration Review Time Frames

Every registration required to be filed with the Commission must be reviewed and issued a certificate of registration in accordance with the following schedule:

A. Comprehensive registration. Registration shall be effective only upon the issuance of a certificate of registration issued by the Commission, which, in the ordinary course of business, should occur no more than sixty (60) calendar days after actual receipt by the state agency of the properly completed application. The Commission must provide a list of deficiencies in the application, if any, and the time for issuance of the certificate of registration by the Commission will be sixty (60) calendar days from receipt by the Commission of the information listed in the deficiencies in the application.

B. Abbreviated registration. Registration shall be effective only upon the issuance of a certificate of registration issued by the Commission, which, in the ordinary course of business, should occur no more than thirty (30) calendar days after receipt by the Commission of the properly completed application. The Commission must provide a list of deficiencies in the application, if any, and the time for issuance of the certificate of registration by the Commission will occur no more than thirty (30) calendar days from receipt by the Commission of the information listed in the deficiencies in the application.

C. Preliminary permit. A preliminary permit shall be issued within twenty (20) calendar days after receipt of a properly completed application, unless the Commission provides to the applicant a list of deficiencies in the application. A preliminary permit shall be issued within fifteen (15) calendar days after receipt by the Commission of the information listed in the deficiencies in the application.

D. The applicant nor a presumption of approval of the application. The Commission may, for cause, extend the approval periods.

Source: Miss. Code Ann. §§ 73-35-35

Rule 8.7 Purchase Contracts

A. Each developer shall furnish each purchaser with a fully completed and executed copy of a contract, which contract shall include the following information:

(1) The actual date the contract is executed by all parties;

(2) The names and addresses of the seller, the developer and the timeshare plan;

(3) The total financial obligation of the purchaser, including the purchase price and any additional charges to which the purchaser may be subject, such as any recurring assessment;

(4) The estimated date of availability of each accommodation, which is not completed;

(5) A description of the nature and duration of the timeshare interest being sold, including whether any interests in real property is being conveyed and the specific number of years or months constituting the term of contract;

(6) Immediately above the signature line of the purchaser(s), the following statement shall be printed in conspicuous type:

You may cancel this contract without any penalty or obligation within seven (7) calendar days from the date you sign this

contract and seven (7) calendar days after you receive the public offering statement, whichever is later. If you decide to cancel this contract, you must notify the developer in writing of your intent to cancel. Your notice of cancellation shall be effective upon the date sent and shall be sent to (name of developer) at (address of developer). If you cancel the contract during a the seven-day cancellation period, the developer shall refund to you all payments made under the contract within thirty (30) days after receipt of your cancellation notice.

No purchaser should rely upon representations other than those included in this contract.

(7) These statements in Paragraph f. may not be waived and failure to include them in a timeshare contract shall render the contract void.

(8) Seller shall refund all payments made by the purchaser under the contract and return all negotiable instruments, other than checks, executed by the purchaser in connection with the contract within 30 days from the receipt of the notice of cancellation transmitted to the developer from the purchaser or if the purchaser has received benefits under the contract, refund all payments made less actual cost of benefits actually received by the purchaser before the date of cancellation, with an accounting of the actual costs of the benefits deducted from payments refunded.

Source: Miss. Code Ann. §§ 73-35-35

Rule 8.8 Exchange Program

A. If a purchaser is offered the opportunity to subscribe to an exchange program, the purchaser should receive written information concerning the exchange program prior to or concurrently with the execution of the contract with the exchange company. Such information should include, without limitation, the following information.

(1) The name and address of the exchange company;

(2) The names of all officers, directors and shareholders of greater that 10% interests of the exchange company;

(3) A description of the purchaser's contractual relationship with the exchange program and the procedure by which changes may be made;

(4) A description of the procedure to qualify for and effectuate changes;

(5) A description of the limitations, restrictions or priority employed in the operation of the exchange program;

(6) The fees or range of fees for participation in the exchange program and the circumstances under which the fees may be changed;

(7) The name and address of each timeshare plan participating in the exchange program;

(8) The number of timeshare interests reported in seven (7) day usage periods in each timeshare plan participating in the exchange progrm; and

(9) The number of purchasers for each timeshare plan participating in the exchange program.

B The exchange program should report on an annual basis following an audit by an independent certified public accountant the following:

(1) The number of purchasers enrolled in the exchange program;

(2) The number of accommodations that have current affiliation

agreements with the exchange program;

(3) The percentage of confirmed reservations;

(4) The number of timeshare periods for which the exchange program has an outstanding obligation to provide an exchange to a purchaser who relinquished a timeshare period during the year; and

(5) The number of exchanges confirmed by the exchange program during the year.

C. No developer shall have any liability with respect to any violation of these rules arising out of the publication by the developer of information provided to it by an exchange company pursuant to this section. No exchange company shall have any liability with respect to any violation of these rules arising out of the use by a developer of information relating to an exchange program other than that provided to the developer by the exchange company.

D. An exchange company may elect to deny exchange privileges to any purchaser whose use of the accommodations of the purchaser's timeshare plan is denied, and no exchange program or exchange company shall be liable to any of its members or any third parties on account of any such denial of exchange privileges.

Source: Miss. Code Ann. §§ 73-35-35 37

Rule 8.9 Escrows and Alternatives Assurances

In order to protect the purchaser's right to refund during the rescission period and during any period in which construction of the timeshare property is not complete and available for occupancy by purchasers, the developer shall provide financial assurances as required by this section.

A. A developer of a timeshare plan shall deposit into an escrow account in an acceptable escrow depository all funds that are received in Mississippi during the purchaser's rescission period. An acceptable escrow depository includes banks, trust companies, saving and loans associations, real estate broker trust accounts at such an institution, title insurers, and underwritten title companies. The handling of these funds shall be in accordance with an executed escrow agreement between an escrow agreement between an escrow agent and the developer. Funds will be handled to assure the following:

(1) Funds may be disbursed to the developer by the escrow agent from the escrow account or from the broker trust account only after expiration of the purchaser's rescission period and in accordance with the purchase contract, subject to paragraph 2.

(2) If a prospective purchaser properly cancels the purchase contract following expiration of the cancellation period pursuant to its terms, the funds shall be paid to the prospective purchaser or paid to the developer if the prospective purchaser's funds have been previously refunded by the developer.

B. If a developer contracts to sell a timeshare interest and the construction of the accommodation in which the timeshare interest being conveyed is located has not been completed, the developer, upon expiration of the rescission period, shall continue to maintain in an escrow account all funds received by or on behalf of the developer from the prospective purchaser under his or her purchase contract. The Commission shall determine the types of documentation which shall be required for evidence of completion, including, but not limited to, a certificate of occupancy, a certificate of substantial completion, or an inspection by the State Fire Marshal or designee or an equivalent public safety inspection by the appropriate agency in the applicable jurisdiction. Unless the developer submits an alternative financial assurance in accordance with paragraph 3., funds shall not be released from escrow until a certificate of occupancy, or its equivalent, has been obtained and the rescission period has passed, and the timeshare interest can be transferred free and clear of blanket encumbrances, including mechanics' liens. Funds to be released from escrow shall be released as follows:

(1) If a prospective purchaser properly cancels the purchase contract pursuant to its terms, the funds shall be paid to the prospective purchaser or paid to the developer if the developer has previously refunded the prospective purchaser's funds. (See "1 boo above)

(2) If a prospective purchaser defaults in the performance of the prospective purchaser's obligations under the purchase contract, the funds shall be paid to the developer.

(3) If the funds of a prospective purchaser have not been previously disbursed in accordance with the provisions of this paragraph 2., they may be disbursed to the developer by the escrow agent upon the issuance of acceptable evidence of completion of construction and closing.

C In lieu of the provisions in paragraphs 1 and 2, the Commission may accept from the developer a surety bond, escrow bond, irrevocable letter of credit, or other financial assurance or arrangement acceptable to the Commission. Any acceptable financial assurances shall be in an amount equal to or in excess of the lesser of

(1) the funds that would otherwise be place in escrow, or

(2) in an amount equal to the cost to complete the incomplete property in which the timeshare interest is located. However, in no event shall the amount be less that the amount of funds that would otherwise be placed in escrow pursuant to subparagraph a. of

paragraph 1.

D. The developer shall provide escrow account or broker trust account information to the Commission and shall execute in writing an authorization consenting to an audit or examination of the account by the Commission. The developer shall make documents related to the escrow or trust account or escrow obligation available to the Commission upon request. The escrow agent or broker shall maintain any disputed funds in the escrow account until either of the following occurs:

(1) Receipt of written direction agreed to by signature of all parties.

(2) Deposit of the funds with a court of competent jurisdiction in which a civil action regarding the funds has been filed

E. Excluding any encumbrance placed against the purchaser's timeshare interest securing the purchaser's payment of purchase money financing for the purchase, the developer shall not be entitled to the release of any funds escrowed under this section J. with respect to each timeshare interest and any other property or rights to property appurtenant to the timeshare interest, including any amenities represented to the purchaser as being part of the timeshare plan, until the developer has provided satisfactory evidence to the Commission of one of the following:

(1) The timeshare Interest together with any other property or rights to property appurtenant to the timeshare interest, including any amenities represented to the purchaser as being part of the timeshare plan, are free and clear of any of the claims of the developer, any owner of the underlying fee, a mortgagee, judgment creditor, or other lien holder, or any other person having an interest in or lien or encumbrance against the timeshare interest or appurtenant property or property rights.

(2) The developer, any owner of the underlying fee, a mortgagee, judgment creditor, or other lien holder, or any other person having an interest in or lien or encumbrance against the timeshare interest or appurtenant property or property rights, including any amenities represented to the purchaser as being part of the timeshare plan, has recorded a subordination and notice to creditors document in the appropriate public records of the jurisdiction in which the timeshare interest is located. The subordination document shall expressly and effectively provide that the interest holder's right, lien or encumbrance shall not adversely affect, and shall be subordinate to, the rights of the owners of the timeshare interests in the timeshare plan regardless of the date of purchase.

(3) The developer, any owner of the underlying fee, a mortgagee, judgment creditor, or other lien holder, or any other person having an interest in or lien or encumbrance against the timeshare interest or appurtenant property or property rights, including any amenities represented to the purchaser as being part of the timeshare plan, has transferred the subject accommodations, amenities, or all use rights in the amenities to a nonprofit organization or owners' association to be held for the use and benefit of the owners of the timeshare plan, which organization or owners association shall act as a fiduciary to the purchasers, and the developer has transferred control of the entity to the owners or does not exercise its voting rights in the entity with respect to the subject accommodations or amenities: Prior to the transfer, any lien or other encumbrance against the accommodation or facility shall be made subject to a subordination and notice to creditors, instrument pursuant to subparagraph b. or be free and clear of all liens and encumbrances.

(4) Alternative arrangements have been made which are adequate to protect the rights of the purchasers of the timeshare interests and approved by the Commission.

F. Nothing in this section shall prevent a developer from accessing any escrow funds if the developer has complied with paragraph 3 of this section.

G. The developer shall notify the Commission of the extent to which an accommodation may become subject to a tax or other lien arising out of claims against other purchasers in the same timeshare plan.

H. Developers, sellers, escrow agents, brokers and their employees and agents have a fiduciary duty to purchasers with respect to funds required to be deposited under these rules. Any Mississippi broker or salesperson who fails to comply with rules concerning the establishment of an escrow or broker trust account, deposits of funds, and property into escrow or withdrawal there from, shall be in violation of the Mississippi Real Estate Brokers Act of 1954, as amended, and the Rules and Regulations of the Commission. The failure to establish an escrow or trust account or to place funds therein as required under these rules is *prima facie* evidence of an intentional and purposeful violation. 40

Source: Miss. Code Ann. §§ 73-35-35

Rule 8.10 Insurance

A. For single site timeshare plans and component sites of multi-site timeshare plans located in this state, the timeshare instrument shall require that the following insurance be at all times maintained in force to protect timeshare interest owners in the timeshare plan:

(1) Insurance against property damage as a result of fire and other hazards commonly insured against, covering all real and personal property comprising the timeshare plan in an amount not less than 80 percent of the full replacement value of the timeshare property.

(2) Liability insurance against death, bodily injury, and property

damage arising out of or in connection with the use, ownership, or maintenance for the accommodations of the timeshare plan. The amounts of the insurance shall be determined by the association, but shall not be less than five hundred thousand dollars ($500,000) to One Million Dollars ($1,000,000) for personal injury and One Hundred Thousand Dollars ($100,000) for property damage.

B. In a timeshare use offering, the trustee, if one exists, shall be a named coinsured, and if for any reason, title to the accommodation is not held in trust, the association shall be named as a coinsured as the agent for each of the timeshare interest owners.

C. In a timeshare estate offering, the association shall be named as a coinsured if it has title to the property or as a coinsured as agent for each of the timeshare interests owners if title is held by the owners as tenants in common.

Source: Miss. Code Ann. §§ 73-35-35

Rule 8.11 Advertising and Marketing:

A. No advertising shall:

(1) Misrepresent a fact or create a false or misleading impression regarding the timeshare plan.

(2) Make a prediction of increases in the price or value of timeshare periods.

(3) Contain any contradictory statements.

(4) Describe any improvements to the timeshare plan that will not be built or that are described as completed when not completed.

B. No promotional device, sweepstakes, lodging certificate, gift award, premium, discount, drawing, prize or display in connection with an offer to sell a timeshare interest may be 41 utilized without the applicable disclosure as follows:

(1) That the promotional device is being used for the purposes of soliciting sales of timeshare periods;

(2) Of the name and address of each timeshare plan or business entity participating in the program;

(3) Of the date and year when all prizes are to be awarded;

(4) Of the method by which all prizes are to be awarded;

(5) If applicable, a statement that it is a national program with multiple sponsors and the gifts offered are not limited solely to customers of said development, but apply also to other developments.

C. The following are not considered to be advertising materials:

(1) Any stockholder communication, financial report, prospectus or other material required to be delivered to owners, prospective purchasers or other persons by an agency of any state or the federal government;

(2) Any communication addressed to and relating to the account of any person who has previously executed a contract for the purchase of a timeshare interest in a timeshare plan to which the communication relates;

(3) Any oral or written statement disseminated to the broadcast, print or other news media, other than paid advertising, regarding plans for the acquisition or development of timeshare property. However, any redistribution of such oral or written statements to a prospective purchaser in any manner would constitute an advertisement;

(4) Any publication or material relating to the promotion of

accommodations for transient rental, so long as a mandatory tour of a timeshare plan or attendance at a mandatory sales presentation is not a term or condition of the availability of such accommodations, so long as the failure of the transient renter to take a tour of a timeshare plan or attend a sales presentation does not result in the transient renter receiving less than what was promised in such materials;

(5) Any audio, written or visual publication or material relating to an exchange company or exchange program providing to an existing member of that exchange company or exchange program.

Source: Miss. Code Ann. §§ 73-35-35

Rule 8.12 Management

A. Before the first sale of a timeshare period, the developer shall create or provide for a managing entity, which may be the developer, a separate management firm, or an owner's association, or some combination thereof.

B. The management entity shall act in the capacity of fiduciary to the purchasers of the timeshare plans.

C. The duties of the management entity shall include, but are not limited to:

(1) Management and maintenance of all accommodations constituting the timeshare plan.

(2) Preparing an itemized annual operating and reserve budget.

(3) The assessment and collection of funds for common expenses.

(4) The assessment and collection of property taxes and casualty insurance and liability insurance against the owners, for which managing entity shall he primarily liable.

(5) Maintenance of all books and records concerning the timeshare plan, and making all of them reasonably available for inspection by any purchaser, or the authorized agent of such purchaser.

(6) Arranging for an annual independent audit to be conducted of all the books and financial records of the timeshare plan by a certified public accountant. A copy of the audit shall be forwarded to the officers of the owner's association; or, if no association exists, the owner of each timeshare period shall be notified in writing that such audit is available upon request.

(7) Scheduling occupancy of the timeshare units so that all purchasers will be provided the use and possession of the accommodations for which they have contracted.

(8) Notifying purchasers of common assessments and the identity of the managing entity.

(9) Performing any other functions and duties that are necessary and proper to maintain the accommodations and operate the owners association as provided in the contract or the timeshare instruments.

(10) Maintaining appropriate insurance as required by Rule 8.9 of these rules.

D. The managing entity shall not be required to provide a reserve budget for any timeshare plan or accommodation for which a timeshare instrument has been approved prior to adoption of these rules. 43

Source: Miss. Code Ann. §§ 73-35-35

Rule 8.13 Liens

A. The management entity has a lien on a timeshare period from the date an assessment becomes due.

B. The management entity may bring an action in its name to foreclose a lien for assessments in the manner a mortgage of real property is foreclosed, and may bring an action to recover a money judgment for the unpaid assessments, or, when no interest in real property is conveyed, an action under the Uniform Commercial Code.

C. The lien is effective from the date of recording in the public records of the county or counties in which the accommodations are located, or as otherwise provided by the laws of the jurisdiction in which the accommodations are located.

D. A judgment in any action or suit brought under this section may include costs and reasonable attorney's fees for the prevailing party.

E. Labor or materials furnished to a unit shall not be the basis for the filing of a lien against the timeshare unit of any timeshare interest owner not expressly consenting to or requesting the labor or materials.

Source: Miss. Code Ann. §§ 73-35-35

Rule 8.14 Owner Referrals

A. Referrals of prospective customers to the developer by any existing timeshare owner shall be permitted, without the owner holding a real estate license and compensation may be paid to the referring owner, only under the following circumstances:

(1) The existing timeshare owner refers no more than twenty (20) prospective customers in any twelve (12) month period; and

(2) The existing timeshare owner limits his or her activities to referring customers to the developer or the developer's employees or agents and does not show, discuss terms or conditions of purchase or otherwise participate in any negotiations with the

purchase of a timeshare interest.

Source: Miss. Code Ann. §§ 73-35-35

Part 1601 Chapter 9: Errors and Omissions Insurance Coverage

Rule 9.1 Administration

A. Invitations to bid on the Errors and Omissions coverage shall be by advertisement published in the appropriate newspaper having state-wide coverage.

B. Selection and approval of the Errors and Omissions Insurance carrier shall be by Commissioners utilizing consultants or committees as deemed appropriate by the Commission.

C. Upon approval of the carrier, invoices shall be sent via First Class Mail to all licensees; including companies and corporations; along with the necessary information describing the various available coverages, the period of coverage and the minimum requirements for independent coverage if desired by a licensee.

D. Coverage shall be a twelve month period beginning October 1, 1994, and continuing thereafter on twelve month basis.

E. Premiums shall be collected by the carrier or the Commission, at the Commission's discretion.

F. The Commission may maintain computer or written records as required for accurate documentation and administration of this program.

Source: Miss. Code Ann. §§ 73-35-35

Rule 9.2 Licensee Status

A. Active licensees not submitting the required premium or

providing the required proof of acceptable independent coverage within 30 days after the due date of the premium shall be placed automatically on inactive status at the end of the 30 day period.

B. Inactive licensees will not be required to pay the premium until changing to active status and the premium will be assessed on a pro rata basis. However, inactive licensees will be invoiced at the beginning of the policy period. They may pay the full premium at that time if they desire.

C. New licensees will be given notice when their license is issued to provide proof of coverage within 30 days of the issuance of license or pay the premium specified on a pro rata basis. Failure to do so will result in their license being changed to inactive status.

Source: Miss. Code Ann. §§ 73-35-35

Rule 9.3 Independent Coverage

A. Licensees having independent coverage shall submit proof of coverage by the beginning of the policy period as set forth above. Any deficiency in supplying proof of coverage must be corrected within no more than 30 days after the beginning of the policy period. Proof of coverage shall be by a "Certificate of 45

Insurance" provided by the independent insurance carrier.

B. Minimum requirements of independent coverage shall be:

(1) Coverage must be for all activities for which a real estate license is required under this Chapter.

(2) A per claim limit is not less than $100,000.00.

(3) The deductible is not more than $2,500.00 per licensee, per claim, for any damages and the deductible is not more than $1,000.00 per licensee, per claim, for defense costs.

(4) The independent insurance carrier shall agree to a non-cancelable policy or provide a letter of commitment to notify the Commission 30 days prior to intention to cancel.

Source: Miss. Code Ann. §§ 73-35-35 46

Title 30: Professions and Occupations

Part 1602: Oral Proceedings & Declaratory Opinions

Part 1602 Chapter 1: Oral Proceedings

Rule 1.1 Scope.

These rules apply to all oral proceedings held for the purpose of providing the public with an opportunity to make oral presentations on proposed new rules and amendments to rules before the Mississippi Real Estate Commission.

Source: Miss. Code Ann. § 25-43-3.104 (Rev. 2010).

Rule 1.2 When Oral Proceedings will be scheduled on Proposed Rules.

The Commission will conduct an oral proceeding on a proposed rule or amendment if requested by a political subdivision, an agency or ten (10) persons in writing within twenty (20) days after the filing of the notice of the proposed rule.

Source: Miss. Code Ann. § 25-43-3.104 (Rev. 2010).

Rule 1.3 Request Format.

Each request must be printed or typewritten, or must be in legible handwriting. Each request must be submitted on standard business letter-size paper (81/2 inches by 11 inches). Requests may be in the form of a letter addressed to the Commission and signed by the requestor(s).

Source: Miss. Code Ann. § 25-43-3.104 (Rev. 2010).

Rule 1.4 Notification of Oral Proceeding.

The date, time and place of all oral proceedings shall be filed with the Secretary of State's office and mailed to each requestor. The oral proceedings will be scheduled no earlier than twenty (20) days from the filing of this information with the Secretary of State.

Source: Miss. Code Ann. § 25-43-3.104 (Rev. 2010).

Rule 1.5 Presiding Officer.

The Commission Administrator or his designee, who is familiar with the substance of the proposed rule, shall preside at the oral proceeding on a proposed rule.

Source: Miss. Code Ann. § 25-43-3.104 (Rev. 2010).

Rule 1.6 Public Presentation and Participation. 47

A. At an oral proceeding on a proposed rule, persons may make oral statements and make documentary and physical submissions, which may include data, views, comments or arguments concerning the proposed rule.

B. Persons wishing to make oral presentations at such a proceeding shall notify the Board at least one business day prior to the proceeding and indicate the general subject of their presentations. The presiding officer in his or her discretion may allow individuals to participate that have not previously contacted the Commission.

C. At the proceeding, those who participate shall indicate their names and addresses, identify any persons or organizations they may represent, and provide any other information relating to their participation deemed appropriate by the presiding officer.

D. The presiding officer may place time limitations on individual oral presentations when necessary to assure the orderly and expeditious conduct of the oral proceeding. To encourage joint oral presentations and to avoid repetition, additional time may be provided for persons whose presentations represent the views of other individuals as well as their own views.

E. Persons making oral presentations are encouraged to avoid restating matters that have already been submitted in writing.

F. There shall be no interruption of a participant who has been given the floor by the presiding officer, except that the presiding officer may in his or her discretion interrupt or end the participant's time where the orderly conduct of the proceeding so requires.

Source: Miss. Code Ann. § 25-43-3.104 (Rev. 2010).

Rule 1.7 Conduct of Oral Proceeding.

A. Presiding Officer - The presiding officer shall have authority to conduct the proceeding in his or her discretion for the orderly conduct of the proceeding. The presiding officer shall:

(1) call proceeding to order;

(2) give a brief synopsis of the proposed rule, a statement of the statutory authority for the proposed rule, and the reasons provided by the Board for the proposed rule;

(3) call on those individuals who have contacted the Commission about speaking on or against the proposed rule;

(4) allow for rebuttal statements following all participant's comments; and

(5) adjourn the proceeding. 48

B. Questions. - The presiding officer, where time permits and to facilitate the exchange of information, may open the floor to questions or general discussion. The presiding officer may question participants and permit the questioning of participants by other participants about any matter relating to that rule-making proceeding, including any prior written submissions made by those participants in that proceeding; but no participant shall be required to answer any question.

C. Physical and Documentary Submissions. - Submissions presented by participants in an oral proceeding shall be submitted to the presiding officer. Such submissions become the property of the Commission and are subject to the Commission's public records request procedure.

D. Recording. - The Commission may record oral proceedings by stenographic or electronic means.

Source: Miss. Code Ann. § 25-43-3.104 (Rev. 2010).

Part 1503 Chapter 2: Declaratory Opinions

Rule 2.1 Scope.

These rules set forth the Mississippi Real Estate Commission's rules governing the form, content and filing of requests for declaratory opinions, and the Commission's procedures regarding the requests. These rules are intended to supplement and be read in conjunction with the provisions of the Mississippi Administrative Procedures Law, which may contain additional information regarding the issuance of declaratory opinions. In the event of any conflict between these rules and the Mississippi Administrative Procedures Law, the latter shall govern.

Source: Miss. Code Ann. § 25-43-2-103 (Rev. 2010).

Rule 2.2. Persons Who May Request Declaratory Opinions.

Any person with a substantial interest in the subject matter may request a declaratory opinion from the Commission by following the specified procedures. A substantial interest in the subject matter means: an individual, business, group or other entity that is directly affected by the Commission's administration of the laws within its primary jurisdiction. Primary jurisdiction of the agency means the agency has a constitutional or statutory grant of authority in the subject matter at issue.

Source: Miss. Code Ann. § 25-43-2-103 (Rev. 2010).

Rule 2.3 Subjects Which May Be Addressed in Declaratory Opinions.

The Commission will issue declaratory opinions regarding the applicability to specified facts of:

A. a statute administered or enforced by the Commission or

B. a rule promulgated by the Commission.

The Commission will not issue a declaratory opinion a statute or rule which is outside the primary jurisdiction of the Commission.

Source: Miss. Code Ann. § 25-43-2-103 (Rev. 2010).

Rule 2.4 Circumstances In Which Declaratory Opinions Will Not Be Issued.

The Commission may, for good cause, refuse to issue, a declaratory opinion. The circumstances in which declaratory opinions will not be issued include, but are not necessarily limited to:

A. Lack of clarity concerning the question presented;

B. There is pending or anticipated litigation, administrative action, or other adjudication which may either answer the question presented by the request or otherwise make an answer unnecessary;

C. The statute or rule on which a declaratory opinion is sought is clear and not in need of interpretation to answer the question presented by the request;

D. The facts presented in the request are not sufficient to answer the question presented;

E. The request fails to contain information required by these rules or the requestor failed to follow the procedure set forth in these rules;

F. The request seeks to resolve issues which have become moot, or are abstract or hypothetical such that the requestor is not substantially affected by the statute or rule on which a declaratory opinion is sought;

G. No controversy exists concerning the issue as the requestor is not faced with existing facts or those certain to arise which raise a question concerning the application of the statute or rule;

H. The question presented by the request concerns the legal validity of a statute or rule;

I. The request is not based upon facts calculated to aid in the planning of future conduct but is, instead, based on past conduct in an effort to establish the effect of that conduct;

J. No clear answer is determinable;

K. The question presented by the request involves the application of a criminal statute or a set of facts which may constitute a crime;

L. The answer to the question presented would require the disclosure of information which is privileged or otherwise protected by law from disclosure;

M. The question is currently the subject of an Attorney General's opinion request or has been answered by an Attorney General's Opinion;

N. A similar request is pending before this agency or any other agency or a proceeding is pending on the same subject matter before any agency, administrative or judicial tribunal, or where such an opinion would constitute the unauthorized practice of law;

O. Where issuance of a declaratory opinion may adversely affect the interests of the State, the Commission or any of their officers or employees in any litigation which is pending or may reasonably be expected to arise;

P. The question involves eligibility for a license, permit, certificate or other approval by the Commission or some other agency, and there is a statutory or regulatory application process by which eligibility for said license, permit, certificate or other approval would be determined.

Source: Miss. Code Ann. § 25-43-2-103 (Rev. 2010).

Rule 2.5 Written Request Required.

Each request must be printed or typewritten, or must be in legible handwriting. Each request must be submitted on standard business letter-size paper (81/2 inches by 11 inches). Requests may be in the form of a letter addressed to the Board.

Source: Miss. Code Ann. § 25-43-2-103 (Rev. 2010).

Rule 2.6 Where to Send Requests.

All requests must be sent to the Commission Administrator, The Mississippi Real Estate Commission: (1) by mail at P.O. Box

12685, Jackson, MS 39236; or (2) delivered to 2506 Lakeland Drive, Suite 300, Flowood, MS 39232; or (3) sent via facsimile to (601 932-2990. All requests must be sent to the attention of Declaratory Opinion Request as follows: ATTN: DECLARATORY OPINION REQUEST

Source: Miss. Code Ann. § 25-43-2-103 (Rev. 2010).

Rule 2.7 Name, Address, and Signature of Requestor.

Each request must include the full name, telephone number and mailing address of the requestor. All requests shall be signed by the person filing the request, who shall attest that the request complies with the requirements set forth in these rules, including but not limited to a full, complete and accurate statement of relevant facts and that there are no related proceedings pending before any other administrative or judicial tribunal. 51

Source: Miss. Code Ann. § 25-43-2-103 (Rev. 2010).

Rule 2.8 Question Presented.

Each request shall contain the following:

A. A clear and concise statement of all facts on which the opinion is requested;

B. A citation to the statute or rule at issue;

C. The question(s) sought to be answered in the opinion, stated clearly;

D. A suggested proposed opinion from the requestor, stating the answers desired by petitioner and a summary of the reasons in support of those answers;

E. The identity of all other known persons involved in or impacted by the described factual situation, including their relationship to the facts, name, mailing address and telephone number; and

F. A statement to show that the person seeking the opinion has a substantial interest in the subject matter.

Source: Miss. Code Ann. § 25-43-2-103 (Rev. 2010).

Rule 2.9 Time for Board Response.

Within forty-five (45) days after the receipt of a request for a declaratory opinion which complies with the requirements of these rules, the Commission shall, in writing:

A. Issue a declaratory opinion regarding the specified statute or rule as applied to the specified circumstances;

B. Decline to issue a declaratory opinion, stating the reasons for its action; or

C. Agree to issue a declaratory opinion by a specified time but not later than ninety (90) days after receipt of the written request.

D. The forty-five (45) day period shall begin running on the first State of Mississippi business day on or after the request is received the Board, whichever is sooner.

Source: Miss. Code Ann. § 25-43-2-103 (Rev. 2010).

Rule 2.10 Opinion Not Final for Sixty Days.

A declaratory opinion shall not become final until the expiration of sixty (60) days after the issuance of the opinion. Prior to the expiration of sixty (60) days, the Commission may, in its discretion, withdraw or amend the declaratory opinion for any reason which is not arbitrary or capricious. Reasons for withdrawing or amending an opinion include, but are not limited to, a determination that the request failed to meet the requirements of these rules or that the opinion issued contains a legal or factual error.

Source: Miss. Code Ann. § 25-43-2-103 (Rev. 2010).

Rule 2.11 Notice by Board to third parties.

The Commission may give notice to any person, agency or entity that a declaratory opinion has been requested, and may receive and consider data, facts arguments and opinions from other persons, agencies or other entities other than the requestor.

Source: Miss. Code Ann. § 25-43-2-103 (Rev. 2010).

Rule 2.12 Public Availability of Requests and Declaratory Opinions.

Declaratory opinions and requests for declaratory opinions shall be available for public inspection and copying in accordance with the Public Records Act and the Commission public records request procedure. All declaratory opinions and requests shall be indexed by name and subject. Declaratory opinions and requests which contain information which is confidential or exempt from disclosure under the Mississippi Public Records Act or other laws shall be exempt from this requirement and shall remain confidential.

Source: Miss. Code Ann. § 25-43-2-103 (Rev. 2010).

Rule 2.13 Effect of a Declaratory Opinion.

The Commission will not pursue any civil, criminal or administrative action against a person who is issued a declaratory opinion from the Commission and who, in good faith, follows the direction of the opinion and acts in accordance therewith unless a court of competent jurisdiction holds that the opinion is manifestly wrong. Any declaratory opinion rendered by the Commission shall be binding only on the Mississippi Real Estate Commission and the person to whom the opinion is issued. No declaratory opinion will be used as precedent for any other transaction or occurrence beyond that set forth by the requesting person.

Source: Miss. Code Ann. § 25-43-2-103 (Rev. 2010). 53

Title 30: Professions and Occupations

Part 1603 Chapter 1: Board Organization

Rule 1.1 Members.

The Mississippi Real Estate Commission consists of five (5) persons who are appointed by the Governor with the advice and consent of the Senate. Each appointee shall have been a resident and citizen of Mississippi for at least six (6) years prior to their appointment and shall have been a real estate broker for at least five (5) years. There shall be at least one (1) Commissioner from each Congressional District, as such Districts are constituted as of July 1, 2002, and one (1) additional Commissioner shall be appointed without regard to residence in any particular Congressional District. Any member of the Commission may be reappointed by the Governor.

The Commission shall organize by selecting from its members a Chairman and may do all things necessary and convenient to promulgate rules and regulations.

Source: Miss. Code Ann. § 73-35-5

GUIDELINES FOR UNLICENSED PERSONAL ASSISTANTS

MREC list of activities that cannot be conducted by an unlicensed personal assistant.

Guidelines for an Unlicensed Personal Assistant

An "Unlicensed Personal Assistant" who works exclusively for a licensee will ordinarily be an employee rather than an independent contractor under Mississippi and Federal tax, unemployment and workers' compensation law. The licensee must follow all applicable laws. The licensee may pay an employee based on a predetermined rate that is agreeable to both parties as long as the assistant's compensation is NOT in any way related to listings or buyers solicited or obtained by the assistant.

The Mississippi Real Estate Commission (MREC) has created a list of activities that cannot be conducted by an unlicensed personal assistant. The list is NOT inclusive and is intended to serve as a guideline.

Unlicensed Assistants may NOT:

1. Independently show properties that are for rent or sale.

2. Host an open house, kiosk, home show booth, fair, or hand out

materials at such functions UNLESS a licensee is present at all times.

3. Preview, inspect, or determine (measure) the square footage of any property unless accompanied by a licensee.

4. Prepare promotional materials or advertising without the review and approval of a licensee and the principal broker.

5. Negotiate, discuss or explain a contract, listing, lease or any other real estate document with anyone outside the brokerage firm.

6. Answer questions concerning properties listed with the firm,

EXCEPT to confirm that a property is listed, to identify the listing broker or sales agent, and to provide such information as would normally appear in a simple, classified newspaper advertisement (location and/or address).

7. Negotiate the amount of rent, security deposit, or other lease provisions in connection with rental property.

8. Open properties for viewing by prospective purchasers, appraisers, home inspectors, or other professionals.

9. Attend pre-closing walk-through or real estate closings unless accompanied by a licensee.

10. Place calls that would require a license such as cold calling, soliciting listings, contacting sellers, buyers or tenants in person or by phone, contacting expired listings, placing marketing calls, or extending open house invitations.

11. Represent themselves as being a licensee or as being engaged in the business of buying, selling, exchanging, renting, leasing, managing, auctioning, or dealing with options on any real estate or the improvement thereon for others.

Typically, unlicensed assistants MAY:

1. Provide "general" information about listed properties such as location, availability, and address (without any solicitation on behalf of the assistant).

2. Perform clerical duties, which may include answering the telephone and forwarding calls.

3. Complete and submit listings and changes to a multiple listing service, type contract forms for approval by the licensee and the principal broker, pick-up and deliver paperwork to other brokers and salespersons, obtain status reports on a loan's progress, assemble closing documents and obtain required public information from governmental entities.

4. Write advertising and promotion materials for approval by the licensee and the principal broker, and arrange to place the advertising.

5. Have keys made for listings and place signs on a listed property.

6. Gather information required for a Broker Price Opinion or a Comparative Marketing Analysis.

7. Schedule appointments for the licensee to show a listed property.

8. May be compensated for their work at a predetermined rate that is not contingent upon the occurrence of a real estate transaction.

Licensees may NOT share commissions with unlicensed persons

who have assisted in transactions by performing any service with respect to a real estate closing.